DEPARTMENT OF THE NAVY
HEADQUARTERS UNITED STATES MARINE CORPS
WASHINGTON, DC 20380-0001

MCO P10150.1
LFS
8 May 92

MARINE CORPS ORDER P10150.1

From: Commandant of the Marine Corps
To: Distribution List

Subj: GARRISON PROPERTY POLICY MANUAL

Encl: (1) Locator Sheet

Reports Required: List, page v

1. Purpose. This Manual prescribes the policy and procedures governing the acquisition, management, and control of garrison property used at Marine Corps bases, air stations, districts, and other independent commands. The information contained in this Manual reflects the current policy in effect to achieve the DoD objective to improve property management. This Manual does not supersede but complements policy in supply and fiscal matters related to garrison property. This document incorporates all applicable Public Laws and Federal Property Management Regulations and consolidates the policy and procedures for Marine Corps garrison property management into a single document. Appendix A provides the references and appendix B the acronyms used in this Manual.

2. Cancellation: MCO 4200.9J, MCO 10160.8B, MCO 10460.2G, MCO 7100.10, MCO 7321.2H, and HQO 11016.1E.

3. Action. Activity commanders reponsible for the management and control of garrison property shall comply with the instructions contained in this Manual.

4. Reserve Applicability. This Manual is applicable to the Marine Corps Reserve.

5. Certification. Reviewed and approved this date.

R. J. WINGLASS
Deputy Chief of Staff
for Installations and Logistics

DISTRIBUTION: PCN 10211002500

Copy to: 7000110 (55)
7000163 (25)
7000162 (3)
7000093, 144/8145005 (2)
7000099/8145001/NAVFACENGCOM/DFAS (1)

LOCATOR SHEET

Subj: GARRISON PROPERTY POLICY MANUAL

Location: ____
(Indicate the location(s) of the copy(ies) of this Manual.)

GARRISON PROPERTY POLICY MANUAL

RECORD OF CHANGES

Log completed change action as indicated.

Change Number	Date of Change	Date Received	Date Entered	Signature of Person Incorporated Change

GARRISON PROPERTY POLICY MANUAL

CONTENTS

GARRISON PROPERTY POLICY MANUAL

REPORTS REQUIRED

	REPORT TITLE	REPORT SYMBOL	PARAGRAPH
I.	PSE Inventory Report	DN-7110-03	2006, 6006.2, 8004.4, App L
II.	MFIP Budget	EXEMPT	3001, 3001.1, 3002.1, 6006, App. L
III.	FPSE Budget	EXEMPT	3002.2, 6006.3, App. L
IV.	Collateral Equipment Requirements (Initial Outfitting) (NAVFAC 4-11010/32)	EXEMPT	4002.3b, 6006.5, App. L
V.	CSE Budget Detailed Plant Equipment Item Exhibit	EXEMPT	6005.4a(1), App. L
VI.	CSE Aggregate Budget Requirements	EXEMPT	6005.4a(2), 6005.4c, App. L
VII.	CSE Status Report	DN-7321-04	6005.4a(3), 6005.5c, 8011.1. App. L
VIII.	Semiannual Plant Account Report	DN-7321-01	8011.2, App. L
IX.	Reconciliation of Plant Account (NAVCOMPT Form 167)	DN-7321-02	8002.1, 8011.3, App. L

GARRISON PROPERTY POLICY MANUAL

CHAPTER 1

GENERAL INFORMATION

GARRISON PROPERTY POLICY MANUAL
CHAPTER 1

GENERAL INFORMATION

1000. INTRODUCTION. Garrison property is all Government personal property used to support the operation of a Marine Corps installation and its tenant activities. This Manual establishes for Marine Corps field activities the authority, responsibility, and basic procedures for use of garrison property. The procedures govern the management, control, budgeting, acquisition, use, maintenance, and disposition of garrison property. This Manual consolidates policy and guidance on garrison property into a single document. FMF deployable equipment assigned to or in the possession of operating forces and moved with the unit when the unit rotates or deploys is not classified or reported as garrison property.

1001. OVERVIEW OF BUDGET CATEGORIES. Garrison property is categorized as either plant property or minor property. The criteria for budget and for accountability purposes are different. Items with a unit cost of $5,000 or more are accounted for as plant property and items with a unit cost under $5,000 are minor property. Centrally-managed garrison mobile equipment (GME), as an exception, is accounted for as plant property. For budget purposes, an item with a unit cost greater than $15,000 is plant property investment equipment and is procured with Procurement, Marine Corps (PMC) funds. Items with a unit cost between $5,000 and $15,000 are plant property, but procured as expense items with Operation and Maintenance, Marine Corps and Operation and Maintenance, Marine Corps Reserve (O&MMC/O&MMCR) funds. Minor property is expense items with a unit cost less than $5,000, procured with O&M funds. Some type items can be either plant or minor property, dependent on acquisition criteria, such as automated data processing equipment (ADPE), training and audiovisual information support (TAVIS), food preparation and serving equipment (FPSE). See chapter 6.

1. Plant Property Programs. Plant or investment property programs include command support equipment (CSE), training and audiovisual equipment, ADPE, warehouse equipment, materials handling equipment (MHE), telephone systems, physical security equipment (PHSE), GME, and some FPSE. Investment property is procured with PMC funds.

2. Minor Property Programs. For budget purposes, minor property programs include personnel support equipment (PSE), FPSE, collateral equipment in military construction (MCON CE), and ADPE. Minor property is procured with O&M funds.

3. Other. Other property, such as the official Marine Corps seal and emblem, relocatable facilities, and office equipment, are not budgeted for in separate programs. They are classified as either plant or minor property and are further described in chapter 5 of this Manual.

1002. QUALITY OF LIFE. Quality of life relates to living and working conditions that affect the welfare or morale of personnel using the facilities. The quality of life of the individual Marine is a primary Marine Corps concern. Quality of life can be enhanced through accessibility to disbursing; administrative support; medical care and food services; and improvements to furnishings and furniture, recreation and club facilities, and security.
Emphasis is being placed on improving personnel support facilities through the allocation of funding for construction and modernization of facilities and furnishings. Headquarters Marine Corps will continue to upgrade the quality of facilities to meet current DoD and Marine Corps standards. The garrison property program is intended not only to support the activity mission and functions, but also to improve living and working conditions, improve the quality of life, and enhance morale and retention.

1003. AUTHORITY. Guidance for garrison property is under the authority of the Secretary of Defense and is delegated to the Department of the Navy (DON) for implementation. DON delegated authority to CMC to implement, administer, and review policy and procedures governing control of garrison property within the Marine Corps. In addition, the General Services Administration (GSA) issues policy and procedures in Federal Property Management Regulations (FPMR) which are government-wide property management regulations.

1004. RESPONSIBILITY. The activity commander or the commander's designee is responsible to implement the policy and procedures in this Manual. Activity commanders are the commanding generals or commanding officers of bases, air stations, districts, or organizations of distinct identity performing a specific support mission or function. The activity commander provides garrison property to support the operations of the headquarters, subordinate units, and tenant organizations.

1005. APPLICABILITY. The policy and procedures in this Manual apply to all activities of the Marine Corps, including the Marine Corps Reserve.

GARRISON PROPERTY POLICY MANUAL

CHAPTER 2

PERSONNEL SUPPORT EQUIPMENT

GARRISON PROPERTY POLICY MANUAL

CHAPTER 2

PERSONNEL SUPPORT EQUIPMENT

2000. GENERAL INFORMATION. PSE is furniture, furnishings, and equipment for existing bachelor enlisted quarters (BEQ) and bachelor officers quarters (BOQ), and furniture and furnishings in administrative offices and messhalls.

1. References. Policy governing the provision of PSE is established by the Offices of the Secretary of Defense and FPMR. Additional policy governing the administration, management, use, maintenance, and operation of BEQ/BOQ facilities is in MCO P11000.22. Additional policy for messhalls is in MCO P10110.14 and MCO P10110.34.

2. Authority. While the CMC (LFS) determines the extent and nature of the PSE program, information in this chapter provides guidelines for activity commanders.

3. Definitions.

a. Furniture. Furniture consists of movable articles normally associated with occupancy.

(1) Household Furniture. Household furniture is property used in areas such as living quarters, reception rooms, lounges, and lobbies. Household furniture includes such items as chairs, sofas, tables, beds, wardrobes, and chests.

(2) Office Furniture. Office furniture is property used in areas such as offices, conference and reception rooms, institutional waiting rooms, lobbies, and libraries. Office furniture includes such items as desks, tables, credenzas, bookcases, coat racks, telephone cabinets, filing cabinets, office safes, partitions, sercurity cabinets, chairs, and sofas.

(3) Messhall Furniture is property used in dining facilities. Messhall furniture includes such items as chairs, tables, booths, and partitions.

b. Furnishings. Furnishings are items necessary to provide a reasonable degree of livability in personnel quarters, as indicated in the table of allowances for BEQ/BOQ specified in appendix D. The term "furnishings" does not include household goods, such as bed, bath and table linens, cutlery, silverware, dishes, and kitchen utensils. Procure these items with local O&M funds, Its does not include air-conditioning units or equipment. Furnishings are provide to BEQ/BOQ, administrative offices, and messhall. When a distinction is necessary between furnishings, furniture, and equipment, the following shall apply:

(1) Household Furnishings. Household furnishings supplement household furniture and add to the comfort or utility of the space assigned. Household furnishings include lamps, mirrors, rugs, shower curtains, and bedspreads.

(2) Office Furnishings. Office furnishings supplement office furniture and augment the utility of the space assigned. The articles include lamps, ash trays, trash receptacles, and rugs.

(3) Messhall Furnishings. Messhall furnishings are articles in the food preparation, galley, or dining area which supplement the messhall and augment the utility of the space assigned. These articles include drapes, signs, and pictures.

c. Equipment. Equipment includes general use items such as clothes washers and dryers, refrigerators, cooking ranges, vacuum cleaners, floor polishers, buffers, ice making machines, copiers, and facsimile machines. (Air-conditioning units and equipment may not procured with PSE funds; see MCO P11000.9.) Administrative office equipment is discussed in chapter 5; messhall equipment is discussed in chapter 3.

d. Summary. The table below indicates location of PSE policy in this Manual:

	BEQ/BOQ	ADMINISTRATIVE OFFICES	MESSHALLS
Furniture	Chapter 2	Chapter 2	Chapter 2
Furnishings	Chapter 2	Chapter 2	Chapter 2
Equipment	Chapter 2	Chapter 5	Chapter 3

2001. DESCRIPTION OF PSE ITEMS. Appendix C describes individual PSE items and guidelines for their authorization.

2002. PSE ALLOWANCES. An allowance represents the general type and amount of PSE that may be provided. An allowance is not an authorization to plan, procure, or furnish a facility in the amount listed. The actual items required are determined after considering such factors as size, design, and decor of the space involved; density of occupancy; built-ins provided; size and design of the items being considered; and other similar factors.

1. Table of Allowances. PSE allowances for BEQ/BOQ are in appendix D. PSE allowances for office furniture are in appendix E. Allowances for messhalls are not specified in a table, but are determined by the number of persons served and the square footage of the messhall.

a. Minimum Quantity. The activity commander shall provide the minimum allowances. These allowances shall be used to determine the requirements for initial outfitting of newly constructed BEQ/BOQ, and in the replacement and augmentation of furniture in existing BEQ/BOQ.

b. Maximum Quantity. The quantity of items prescribed for existing facilities may be increased up to the maximum allowances at the discretion of the activity commander provided appropriated funds are available, sufficient space exists, and the rank of the occupant warrants the increase. The activity commander should insure that all occupants have the minimum allowance before providing the maximum allowance for any specific group(s) of occupants.

c. Overfurnishing. Activity commanders shall not procure the maximum allowances without undertaking a space and furniture placement analysis to assure against overfurnishing.

2. Allowance Change Requests (ACR). Facilities shall not be furnished in excess of the quantities and kinds of item allowances without prior approval of CMC (LFS). When the authorized allowance quantities are inadequate to furnish unusually large rooms, an ACR may be submitted. The ACR should include a complete justification and a drawing showing the layout of the room and placement of furniture now on hand. The CMC (LFS) may approve waivers for certain high public visibility situations, such as Marine Corps district headquarters or recruiting stations.

3. PSE Reserve. Only limited amounts of PSE, in addition to those in use or planned for use, are permitted. The PSE reserve shall not be include in the intitial outfitting (MCON CE) requirements, but

should be an augmented quantity, or derived from changes in occupancy needs. The reserve should be determined as follows:

a. Equipment. An addition of 3 percent, by item, of household equipment may be held to allow for circumstances created when repairs are required and for delays involved in obtaining replacements.

b. Furniture. An addition of 5 percent, by item, of furniture may be held to allow for circumstances created when repairs are required and for delays involved in obtaining replacements.

2003. GENERAL CONSIDERATIONS. General guides for selecting PSE are:

1. Planning Requirements. Determine PSE requirements using systematic, detailed, room-by-room planning surveys, taking into account room size, design, decor, architectural innovations, door and window placements, density of occupancy, design of the items being considered, and experience-use records.

2. Environment. Do not institutionalize quarters. Furnish quarters with comfortable, yet durable home-like PSE. Consider preferences of BEQ/BOQ residents, submitted through advisory councils when PSE is procured for upgrade or modernization. Obtain sample items for wear /use testing, before placing large orders.

3. Compatibility. PSE procured for upgrade or replacement should be compatible for use with existing PSE in new or existing facilities.

4. Appropriateness. PSE must be appropriate to the climate and to the particular facility for which it is procured. PSE for areas open to public use, such as in reception areas, should be in harmony with furnishings in the surroundings areas and in keeping with the overall decor. PSE generally used for offices should not be furnished for living quarters or lounges and vice versa.

5. Quality. PSE should be of good quality and within the price ranges for the occupancy category. All PSE should be simple, interchangeable, adaptable, and durable.

6. Material. Carefully select the appropriate material for PSE in each project. Before selection, consider past use experience, climatic factors, and available repair facilities. The expertise and physical resources necessary for periodic minor repairs may be more readily available for one material than for another. The variety of wood and metal furniture and furnishing items available in the Federal Supply Schedule (FSS), from prison industries, and in the GSA supply catalog, should be the first sources considered for procurement. See paragraph 7002 for other selection criteria.

a. Wood Furniture. Wood furniture, the most attractive to purchase, is recommended for use in BEQ/BOQ and executive offices. Solid wood furniture, under normal use, may be subject to more breakage than metal furniture. The optimum benefits of wood furniture that is durable, feasible to refurbish, and compatible with the standard styles of existing PSE will actually minimize life cycle acquisition cost. Wood furniture is acceptable when dowels and corner blocks or braces secured with screws are used at critical points and when the frames are well frames are well constructed and sturdy. Table tops and tops of all drawers units should be high-pressure laminated plastic. Wood furniture is recommended for use in the BEQ/BOQ environment to lessen the institutional appearance.

b. Metal Furniture. Metal furniture, though not as attractive as wood furniture, is generally more durable. When buying for the office and messhall environment, metal furniture of good welded construction is recommended. Seating items with aluminum frame, bolted-type construction, available from GSA FSS, are not durable and are not recommended.

c. Wrought Iron Furniture. Wrought iron furniture is not recommended for use in quarters. Restrict use to exterior applications where the furniture will be exposed to the elements. Other types of outdoor furniture are available in the FSS and should be considered.

7. Personally Owned Furnishings

a. Government -Owned Quarters. Government-owned PSE is provided for all BEQ/BOQ. Personally owned furnishings may be used in BEQ/BOQ in lieu of Government-owned PSE when desired. Washers and dryers shall be provided as delinested in appendix C.

b. Office-Base Quarters. Government-owned PSE is not available for personnel use in off-base quarters. When Marines live in off-base quarters, the responsibility to furnish such quarters rests with the Marine.

c. Storage. Personally-owned PSE transported at Government expense when Government-owned PSE is provided. The PCS allowance for accompanied overseas duty normally does not adequately cover shipment of household goods. Long-time storage of personnel effects is not available overseas. The joint Federal Travel Regulations (JFTR) provides further detail.

2004. OFFICE FURNITURE AND FURNISHINGS

1. Goal. The activity property control office (PCO) shall consolidate requirements for administrative offices. The goal for furnishing these offices is to:

a. Select office furniture and equipment best suited for the operation to improve the efficiency, effectiveness, and productivity of all personnel.

b. Minimize the kinds, types, and sizes of offices furniture and equipment used to economize and facilitate procurement and maintenance.

c. Select economical office furniture and equipment appropriate for each staff level.

2. Office Furniture

a. Level of Office Furniture. FPMR defines three levels of furniture assignments for individuals, including grade limitations.

(1) Level A, Executive. The use of executive office furniture, whether new, used, or rehabilitated, is limited to personnel of flag rank, senior executive service, colonel, grade 15, or above. Level A furniture includes all executive wood furniture consisting of, or comparable to, the traditional and modern wood office furniture and related items illustrated in the GSA Supply Catalog and listed in FSS Federal Supply Class (FSC) Group 71, part IIA.

(2) Level B, Middle Management. The use of middle management office furniture, whether new, used, or rehabilitated, is limited to major/lieutenant colonel or General Schedule (GS) grades 13 and 14 personnel. Level B furniture includes all items of unitized wood office furniture and related items illustrated in the GSA Supply Catalog and listed in, or comparable to, FSS FSC Group 71, part IIB.

(3) Level C, General. The use of general office furniture, whether new, used, or rehabilitated, is authorized for captain and below personnel. Level C furniture includes all contemporary steel, general steel, and general wood office furniture in GSA Supply Catalog.

b. Office Furniture for Support Staff. Secretaries and staff assistants whose duties are in direct support of an executive or manager may be assigned office furniture that is similar or matching that of their executive or manager when they are located in directly adjoining spaces. Staff support personnel in space not immediately adjoining the executive or manager shall be provided furniture commensurate with their work assignment grade.

c. System Furniture. System furniture may be used for managerial, professional, or clerical workstations if the allowed space for the current organizations is inadequate or for expansion requirements. Activities shall carefully determine electrical telephone, and data transmission requirements during the initial layout of the prototypical workstation design. Refer all scope of work or installation sequence changes to the contracting officer for approval. Office system furniture or workstation clusters include furniture system items and related items illustrated in the GSA Supply Catalog and listed in, or comparable to FSS FSC Group 71, part IIE. Appendix E provides typical manager, professional, and clerical workstations layout.

d. Compliance. The IRBAR for each office space indicate if existing furniture does not comply with the assigned furniture level. The PCO will redistribute furniture from spaces that do not rate the furniture level or specific items to spaces that do rate that level or the items. The transfer will occur after the present occupant vacates the area. If on-hand PSE is not available to provide the assigned furniture level or allowance, include the requirements in the activity requirements for augmentation.

3. Office Furnishing. Office furnishings compatible with office furniture are subject to the same grade limitations as office furniture, except that carpet may be supplied for use by personnel of other ranks or in other areas when it is justified and authorized as directed in appendix C. Procure new office furniture for upgrade or replacement only after complying with the criteria described in chapter 7 of this Manual.

4. Office Furniture in the National Capital Region (NCR). The NCR includes the District of Columbia; Montgomery and Prince George's counties in Maryland; Arlington, Fairfax, Loundon, and Prince William counties in Virginia; and the cities of Alexandria, Fairfax, and Falls Church in Virginia. The procurement, storage, and control of office furniture in the NCR are consolidated under the Defense Supply Service-Washington (DSS-W). This consolidation does not apply to household furniture.

a. Applicability. This section applies to all DoD activities in the NCR that are in Government-owned or -leased administrative space, either the control of GSA or DoD.

b. Reference. Policy for the procurement of standard office furnishings for activities in the NCR is FPMR. Federal Acquisition Regulations (FAR) and MCO P4200.15 direct maximum use of GSA stock items listed in the Furniture Catalog, GSA FSS.

c. Replacement Stock. New lines or units adopted as Dod standard office furnishings for the NCR shall be phased in as existing stocks are depleted. DoD activities in the NCR, serviced by DSS-W, shall use available on-hand stock furnishings to meet requirements. Replacement of existing furnishings may be scheduled after considering the remaining economic life and the extended life through reconditioning. Usable office furniture should be concentrated in one area thereby extending its life and maintaining a suitable decor.

2005. INVENTORY, REQUIREMENTS, BUDGET AND REPLACEMENT (IRBAR) PLAN. The IRBAR plan was designed to replace or refurbish PSE in BEQ/BOQ rooms on a rotation basis every 7 years but not to exceed 10 years.

1. Applicability. This policy applies to all Marine Corps activities with management responsibility for BEQ/BOQ.

2. Responsibility. The PCO, as property administrator, has the following responsibilities for PSE:

a. Program Management. The PCO shall develop and plan a PSE program to ensure habitable BEQ/BOQ for residents. A continuing PSE improvement program shall be implemented to repair, replace, augment, or refurbish the PSE inventory. The program goal shall be attain and maintain the established minimum PSE allowances achieved through efforts coordinated with the responsible officers (RO). The PCO shall establish amplifying local guidance for PSE inventory, control, and accountability to comply with applicable supply, maintenance, and fiscal policy.

b. Budget. The PCO, in coordination with each RO, shall develop and implement a PSE refurbishment program on a "whom room" concept. An inventory and budget to support the requirements shall be submitted to CMC (LFS), through the activity comptroller or fiscal officer, annually before 15 September, in the format entitled "PSE Annual Inventory Report," shown in appendix L and as delineated in chapter 6 of this Manual.

c. Standardize PSE. The PCO shall receive requirements input from RO's to determine standard items for procurement. Ro's shall consult and coordinate with the PCO responsible to procure all PSE. Tenants shall not procure PSE independent of the PCO. Tenants may transfer funds to the PCO to procure PSE for emergency requirements.

3. Minimum Standards of Adequacy. The Minimum Standards of Adequacy (MSA) are in DoD 4165.63M. These standards, shown in appendix F, describe the net living area and accommodations allowed per person. Military construction (MILCON) BEQ/BOQ projects follow these standards. Typical room and furniture layouts are shown in figures 1 and 2 in appendix F.

4. BEQ/BOQ Occupancy Plan. The activity shall develop a BEQ/BOQ occupancy plan using the minimum standards of adequacy as a guide to determine the number of personnel housed in each room. The table of allowances for each BEQ/BOQ in appendix D shall be used to determine the PSE requirements for augmentation, replacement, or refurbishment.

5. Schedule. The IRBAR plan provides for PSE replacement or refurbishment on a 7-year planning cycle. Time, funds, and occupancy requirements may require up to 10 years to complete the plan. The number of rooms, lounges, and miscellaneous areas for refurbishment should be one-seventh to one-tenth the total BEQ/BOQ capacity. PSE should be scheduled for repair, however, when needed. Acceptable PSE from each year's IRBAR plan and PSE the PCO has on hand should be used to upgrade the BEQ/BOQ as needed. Remaining PSE requirements should be augmented with new PSE.

6. "Whole Room" Basis. Schedule PSE refurbishment on a "whole room" basis. Replace PSE on a room-by-room, floor-by-floor basis, allowing for the established minimum allowance and size of the refurbished room. All furniture, new and on-hand, should be listed for each room. Use only new or new-condition furniture. Schedule renovation (painting, etc.) simultaneously to ensure "new" rooms are being created.

7. IRBAR Record keeping. Documentation of PSE placed in BEQ/BOQ under the IRBAR plan is maintained on the IRBAR plan format shown in appendix L. Use file for each facility at each activity and/or RO to complete the IRBAR plan. Set up and tab the file to show each fiscal year's PSE acquisition by room and building number. Maintain and update, at the time of annual inventory, the master chart to show the total BEQ/BOQ by room and date of last PSE replacement and renovation. Include the proposed renovation for the next year on this master chart. Reconcile inventory results with accountability records. Maintain the permanent file of PSE placed in BEQ/BOQ with the BEQ/BOQ manager or PCO, as designated. Use an automated application to manage the program data base.

8. Office and Messhall Furniture. A separate IRBAR plan shall be prepared and submitted for administrative offices and messhalls to develop PSE requirements. The office IRBAR plan shall provide for replacement or refurbishment of one-tenth the office furniture each year. The minimum standard of adequacy for office spaces indicated in FPMR for Government-owned space is an average of 135 ft per workstation including supplemental space. Where system furniture is used, the goal is 122 ft. Use an automated spreadsheet application to manage the program database.

2006. BUDGET REQUIREMENTS. PSE for BEQ/BOQ's, administrative office, and messhalls is funded from Headquarters-managed PSE program and local funds, if available. The inventory and statement of dollars obligated and budgeted in the procurement of PSE is reported on the PSE Annual Inventory Report (RCS-DN-7110-03), shown in appendix L. This report is generated from the IRBAR Plan. The PSE Annual Inventory Report is submitted to CMC (LFS) before 15 September each year. The report is used to formulate the annual allocation plan for each activity and is the basis for future PSE budget submission at the CMC level.

GARRISON PROPERTY POLICY MANUAL

Chapter 3

FOOD PREPARATION AND SERVING EQUIPMENT

CHAPTER 3

FOOD PREPARATION AND SERVING EQUIPMENT

3000. GENERAL INFORMATION. The FPSE program provides major equipment support for messhalls at major continental Untied States (CONUS) and overseas installations. FPSE refers to all major equipment used in messhall galleys, serving and dining areas, food services schools, and officers' field ration messhalls (OFRM), which are general messes for unaccompanied officers. Typical items are ovens, dishwashers, refrigerators, grills, beverage dispensers, slicers, and food mixers.

1. Reference. Complete guidelines governing the food service program are in MCO P10110.14.

2. Exclusions

a. PSE. Furniture or furnishings, defined as PSE, required for replacement or augmentation purposes in messhalls is not included in the FPSE program. Messhall PSE is included in the PSE program (chapter 2 of this Manual).

b. MCON CE. The CMC (LFS) shall program for the initial outfitting requirements of new construction projects for messhalls based on documents submitted for MCON CE projects (chapter 4 of this Manual).

c. Expendable Items. For budget purposes, cutlery, dishes, glassware, napkins, tablecloths, utensils, fast food paper products, and other such expendable items are not considered FPSE. Procure these items with local O&M funds.

d. Procurement. FPSE is normally procured through the DoD supply system. Submit requisitions to Defense General Supply Center (S9G), Richmond, Virginia. The lead time will vary depending on stock availability or the need to award a contract. When special requirements exist, such as emergency replacement, equipment with special features, or contractor installation, procure this FPSE commercially using the guidance in chapter 7 of this Manual.

3001. MESSHALL FACILITY IMPROVEMENT PROGRAM. The Messhall Facility Improvement Program (MFIP) is designed to improve the unity and upgrade the appearance of messhalls throughout the Marine Corps. Evaluate all messhalls on a 5- to 6-year rotation basis to determine MFIP requirements. Use the IRBAR plan described in chapter 2 of this Manual to identify the decor and equipment for replacement or refurbishment.

1. Funding. MFIP projects are funded on a turnkey basis with a combination of O&MMC, MILCON, and PMC appropriations, as appropriate.

2. Projects. MFIP projects should include funding requirements for minor construction or repair, expense and investment equipment requirements, a decor package, and installation costs. Submit MFIP projects for each budget year to CMC (LFS) before 15 March each year, in the format entitled "Messhall Facility Improvement Program (MFIP) Project requirements," shown in appendix L.

a. Minor Construction or Repair. Submit requirements for minor construction or repair as directed in MCO P11000.5.

b. Expense and Investment Equipment. Expense equipment requirements for normal replacement are included in the FPSE budget, while investment equipment replacement requirements are included in the CSE planet property budget. Food service office at each installation shall ensure a folder, based on the Maintenance Equipment Replacement Record in MCO P10110.14, is kept to record the maintenance history for each piece of expense and investment equipment. This information shall be used to assist with replacement decisions and project a reasonable life expectancy for new equipment.

c. Decor Package. The decor package includes furniture and furnishings such as drapes, pictures, plants, and accessories required to upgrade messhall to standards comparable with commercial dining establishments.

d. Installation Costs. Installation and transportation costs are listed in addition to the equipment costs are listed in addition to the equipment costs. Installation shall be funded from the same appropriation used to procure the equipment. When installation is specified in the contract, installation costs shall be included in the project for the equipment, whether Government-furnished and contractor-installed, or contractor-furnished and contactor-installed on a turnkey basis.

3002. BUDGET REQUIREMENTS

1. MFIP Projects. Activities submit MFIP projects annually for the budget year, and for 1 additional year, to the CMC (LFS/LFF) through the activity comptroller or fiscal officer in the format entitled "Messhall Facility Improvement Program (MFIP) Budget," shown in appendix L. This report is exempt from reports control. Activities submit regular FPSE requirements as specified in chapter 6.

2. FPSE Requirements for Messhalls. FPSE are allocated to each activity based on the available funds and the FPSE requirements for each budget year in the format entitled "Food Preparation and Serving Equipment Requirements for Messhalls," shown in appendix L.

GARRISON PROPERTY POLICY MANUAL

CHAPTER 4

COLLATERAL EQUIPMENT IN MILITARY CONSTRUCTION

CHAPTER 4

COLLATERAL EQUIPMENT IN MILITARY CONSTRUCTION

4000. GENERAL INFORMATION. Collateral equipment in military construction (MCON CE), also known as initial outfitting, is the first provision of furniture, furnishing, and equipment for a requirement generated through new construction or expansion of a facility. Project performed in conjunction with a military construction (MILCON), unspecified minor construction (UMC), or a Government of Japan, Japanese Facility Improvement Program (JFIP) will result in a change in function or operation, or an improvement in the physical condition of the facility.

1. Reference. Policy addressing facility construction and collateral equipment programs is in MCO P11000.12. This chapter supplements those instructions as related to the timely preparation and submission of MILCON listings. These guidelines apply to all new construction projects and projects involving conversion or modernization of existing space.

2. Authorization. The CMC (LFS) will approve all projects for procurement of furniture, furnishings, and equipment for newly constructed facilities (e.g., BEQ/BOQ, messhall, training, armory, maintenance, chapel, and other facilities) as collateral equipment for MILCON, UMC, and JFIP projects, subject to the required certification. Procurement authorization for each MCON CE project will be delegated to the user activities.

4001. EXCLUSIONS

1. Budget Shortages. Outfitting a new MILCON, UMC, or JFIP facility is not intended as a means to overcome furniture, furnishings, or equipment deficiencies, or to replace on-hand serviceable or unserviceable items that should be supported from operating budgets.

2. Table of Equipment (T/E) Allowance Items. T/E items will not be included on the list. Equipment used to augment T/E allowances for FMF tenants while operating in the garrison environment may be included, if necessary, for that particular MILCON, JFIP, or UMC project. Commercial items which duplicate a T/E item function shall not be procured if the purpose is to avoid using the T/E item while in the garrison environment.

4002. BUDGET. When planning any building, prepare a realistic and complete collateral equipment budget to develop a totally integrated and useful facility.

1. Project Engineering Documentation. The activity commander will be notified once the CMC requests the Commander, NAval Facilities Engineering Command (NAVFACENGCOM) to develop and prepare the project engineering documentation (PED). At that time, the activity commander must then provide feeder data to the NAVFACENGCOM Engineering Field Division (EFD) preparing the PED. In doing this, the input from the activity commander is available at the start of the PED development and is not limited to reaction to an already completed document.

2. Interior Design Services. Activity commanders should use the interior design services as indicated in NAVFACINST 11010.74. NAVFACENGCOM maintains professional staff interior design capability and these services should be used to the extent available, subject only to the NAVFACENGCOM workload for primary new construction. Marine Corps activities are encouraged to solicit interior design assistance from the appropriate NAVFACENGCOM EFD. Such assistance may range from short-term consultation to development of complete

interior design programs. Projects to upgrade BEQ/BOQ, administrative offices, and messhalls are candidates for these services.

3. Documentation. The facility branch or division at each activity will prepare and submit the supporting documentation for construction projects. The supporting documentation specified in MCO P11000.12 includes several major components. In addition to that guidance, the following specific requirements apply to this Manual.

a. DD Form 1391. Military Construction Project Data (DD Form 1391) must be completed accurately. This form is a program and budget document to support the MILCON project. The following specific guidance applies:

(1) Block 10, Description of Proposed Construction. For BEQ/BOQ projects, indicate the grade mix of personnel (e.g., enlisted, officer, or transient) who will occupy the facility.

(2) Block 11, Requirement. Indicate the type of facility and the scope of the project. The survival of the project depends on the contents of this block. Once Congress authorizes the project, it cannot be changed appreciably without additional congressional authorization.

b. Collateral Equipment Requirements (Initial Outfitting) Form. For each project, complete a separate Collateral Equipment Requirements (Initial Outfitting) listing (NAVFAC-4-22020/32), shown in appendix L. Submit this list along with the DD Form 1391 as a PED document. This list documents initial outfitting requirements and funding responsibilities per NAVFACINST 11010.74 and the NavCompt Manual, paragraph 075361. The list helps ensure sufficient funding is available to procure furniture, furnishings, and equipment to meet the beneficial occupancy date (BOD).

(1) Initial and Final Forms. The NAVFAC-4-11010/32 is completed in two phases, known as the initial collateral equipment list and the final collateral equipment list. The initial collateral equipment list is not required to identify national stock numbers (NSN's) or source of supply for "common collateral equipment; " i.e., furniture and furnishings. This data shall be provided subsequent to congressional approval of the project when the construction contract has been awarded. After the activity forwards the initial submission, the collateral equipment list is updated and forwarded to CMC (LFS) the month following any significant changes, such as a revised BOD or change in project scope.

(a) Shopping List. To facilitate funding and procurement, each NAVFAC-4-11010/32 must include a shopping list, indicating each generic item to be provided. This information is expanded from the initial list. Each sheet shall contain information necessary for procurement, installation, and the following:

1 Description.

2 Sizes.

3 Colors/fabrics/materials.

4 Item identification location code.

5 Cost estimates (unit price and total cost).

6 Sources (firm names, addresses, and telephone numbers).

7 Stock numbers/special item number.

8 Contact numbers.

9 Location (type of room).

(b) Floor Plans. Each NAVFAC-4-11010/32 list must include layouts by space or type of room for the various areas of the facility to assure the equipment requirement correlates with the planned occupancy and the available space.

(2) Submission. All activities shall forward refined MCON CE lists (NAVFAC 4-11010/32) for the budget year (BY) to the CMC (LFS), through the activity comptroller of fiscal officer, before 15 March each year. The PCO will coordinate with the public works office charged with the project to develop the refined MCON CE list. UMC and JFIP projects should also be submitted at this time. Activities must submit a duplicate copy of the list for any items funded from other appropriations, such as ADPE or TAVSA, to the specific appropriation sponsor as indicated in appendix L. A duplicate copy of the initial list should be forwarded to the cognizant appropriation sponsor to facilitate planning and budgeting.

4003. FUNDS. O&MMC or O&MMCR funds will be provided in the activity operating budget fund authorization to procure approved expense items. PMC funds will be provided from the applicable equipment appropriation in a letter of authorization and a allotment document. PMC investment funds will be provided for approved Military Construction Naval Reserve (MCNR) projects. The funds will be provided 180 to 270 days before the BOD to allow sufficient time to procure the collateral equipment.

CHAPTER 5

OTHER PROPERTY

5000. GENERAL INFORMATION. This chapter addresses garrison property not previously addressed as PSE, FPSE, or MCON CE. Included are automated data processing equipment (ADPE); child care facilities equipment; cranes; garrison mobile equipment (GME);interim relocatable facilities; morale, welfare, and recreation (MWR) equipment; office equipment; physical security equipment(PHSE); the official Bronze Marine Corps seal and emblem; training and audiovisual equipment; uninterrupted power supply (UPS); and warehouse equipment. Information herein relates only to the garrison environment. Further information about specific programs can be found in the references.

5001. AUTOMATED DATA PROCESSING EQUIPMENT. ADPE includes ADPE, word processing equipment (WPE), and office information systems equipment (OISE).

1. Applicability. The policy and procedures of this section apply to all operating forces within FMF units, using ADPE/WPE/OISE both for deployment and for garrison operations, and for the supporting establishment (SE) using ADPE/WPE/OISE in garrison operations.

2. Scope. Additional commercially available ADPE has been procured for dual use both in garrison and in deployed situations to offset the shortfall of ADPE-FMF "green machines" or end-user computer equipment (EUCE). Safeguards are required for the security and accountability of this type commercial ADPE/WPE/OISE (as opposed to the ADPE-FMF "green machine" or EUCE). This ADPE/WPE/OISE is not classified as a tactical weapon system. Because of the equipment diversity, the lack of standardization, and the dynamic advances of technology, tables of allowances were introduced after the equipment was put into use. The procedures for multi-functional use in both environments have been simplified and control standards established.

3. Supporting Establishment Procedures. All ADPE/WPE/OISE used only in the SE, which meet the plant property expense/investment criteria defined in chapter 6 of this Manual, shall comply with the procedures to manage and control class 3 plant property. The remaining ADPE/WPE/OISE equipment used only in the SE is considered minor property and shall also comply with accountability procedures delineated in chapter 8 of this Manual.

4. FMF and Reserve Procedures. FMF Active and Reserve commanders shall inventory all ADPE/WPE/OISE annually to identify both equipment for operation in garrison only and equipment for operation during deployment and in garrison. Equipment designated for operation in garrison only shall be accounted and budgeted for as delineated in chapters 6 and 8 of this Manual. FMF units shall not record garrison equipment on the unit accountability files.

a. FMF Property Control. Control of ADPE/WPE/OISE designated for the FMF shall comply with applicable procedures for documentation, property identification, budgeting, maintenance, and property management as delineated in MCO P4400.150.

b. Transit Containers. The design and construction of transit containers shall comply with MIL-C-4150 to provide adequate protection during shipment and storage. FMF commanders shall budget and fund for the resources necessary to provide the required containers.

5. Allowances. FMF commanders shall establish ADPE/WPE/OISE allowances for existing equipment based on need as delineated in MCO P5230.10.

6. Table of Authorized Material Control Number (TAMCN) Assignment. Equipment designated for use, in deployment and garrison operations, shall be assigned a local TAMCN at the local command level. The stock number and data for each piece of equipment shall be added to the loaded unit allowance file (LUAF) and/or mechanized allowance list (MAL). Local TAMCN's shall be assigned according to procedures in UM 4400-15 and UM 4400-124, and the codes shown in appendix H.

7. Procedures. FMF commanders shall use the following procedures to assign TAMCN's:

a. Load all on-hand quantities of equipment designated deployable to the LUAF.

b. Load quantities and serial numbers to the reporting unit allowance file (RUAF).

c. Report the remaining garrison property not designated deployable to the host plant account or activity property control office (PCO) for tagging and preparation of the property record.

d. Identify FMF allowance deficienies, with justification for inclusion in the budget and programming process. Submit garrison property requirements through budget procedures the activity commander designates to comply with chapter 6 of this Manual.

8. Reporting. All FMF units must submit reports (RCS MC-5233-02) of receipted ADPE/WPE/OISE equipment. Units shall use the data processing installation codes (DPIC) shown in appendix M to report ADPE (hardware and software). To comply with DoDDir 7950.1-M, the MCCTA (CTAR) will consolidate the reports, manage the inventory, have cognizance of disposition actions, budget and fund for O&MMC and PMC requirements, and track replacement of equipment through the serial number. The CMC (LFS) shall monitor all equipment designated as plant and minor property.

9. Peripheral Equipment. The CMC (LFS) will consolidate budget submissions for all related PMC peripheral equipment requirements, not classified as ADP (FSC 70), but classified as class 3 plant property in the NavCompt Manual, volume 3, chapter 6.

5002. CHILD CARE FACILITIES. A Child Development Center (CDC) is funded as an MWR activity. The CDC is designed to provide developmental child care services for military families.

1. Reference. Policy and standards related to the CDC program are in the MCO 1710.30.

2. Funding. The initial outfitting of a CDC shall comply with the policy in chapter 4 of this Manual. The CE list should identify the different equipment categories and comply with the CDC equipment standards in MCO 1710.30. CMC (LFS) will provide MCON CE funds after CMC (MH) reviews and evaluates each CDC MILCON project against current CDC collateral equipment requirements. Funds for each project will depend on funds available in the MCON CE program and any MWR thresholds in effect at the time.

5003. CRANES. Cranes and crane operating mechanisms are classified as personal property rather than real property. The crane runway within a building or structure and extending from within the building or structure is defined as class 2 real property. Mobile cranes carried under the GME program (paragraph 5004) are the exception.

5004. GARRISON MOBILE EQUIPMENT (GME). GME is equipment used to perform transportation and automotive maintenance functions at Marine Corps facilities. Commercially available GME includes passenger vehicles, cargo vehicles, material handling equipment, engineer equipment, and railway rolling stock. GME is not for tactical use.

1. Reference. Guidance on administrative and technical instructions, policy, and procedures for all personnel involved in the management, procurement, operation, and maintenance of GME is in MCO P11240.106.

2. General. The characteristics below apply to all GME and distinguish GME from other garrison property.

a. Wheeled or Tracked Equipment. The essential characteristic that clearly identifies GME is wheels or tracks. Equipment similar to GME that does not move its own power and/or is not wheeled or tracked equipment is not GME. For example, generators (skid or trailer mounted) or insecticide fogger units are not GME but plant or minor property as shown in appendix K.

b. Centrally Managed. The GME program is centrally managed at HQMC (LFS).

c. PMC Funded. GME is acquired with PMC funds.

d. Includes Table of Authorized Material (TAM)-Controlled Items. All TAM-controlled items listed in MCO P11240.106 are GME and can be procured only with PMC funds.

e. Authorized by CMC (LFS). CMC (LFS) controls and approves all GME allowances.

f. Registration Number. All GME must be assigned a registration number.

g. "USMCGM" Registration Number. All GME is classified as plant property. However, the separate identification format used for GME is "USMCGM" plus the registration number. Further instructions for marking and recording property are in chapter 8 of this Manual.

5005. INTERIM RELOCATABLE FACILITIES. A portable or interim relocatable facility is a building or structure designed to be moved from one location to another, and intended to stay in one location for use of 3 years or less.

1. Classification. A portable or interim relocatable facility is classified and controlled as personal plant property. However, if the building is authorized for procurement with MCON funds, then it is accounted for as real property and added to the Facilities Inventory and Planning System. The expense and investment criteria in chapter 6 of this Manual apply to this facility. Specifically, interim relocatable facilities may be included in the CSE plant property budget if the procedures addressed in MCO P11000.12 are met. However, actual funding depends on the priority the activity assigns the facility in the budget and available funds.

2. Reference. Additional policy and procedures for the acquisition of interim relocatable facilities are in MCO P11000.12.

5006. MORALE, WELFARE, AND RECREATION EQUIPMENT

1. General. The nature of the individual MWR activity determines whether the activity is operated and maintained with appropriated or nonappropriated funds (NAF). Appropriated fund (APF) support can be provided for initial outfitting or replacement dependent on the type MWR activity. Threshold limits may constrain the actual funds available for APF support.

2. Reference. NavCompt Manual, volume 7, paragraph 075500, provides guidance for APF support of recreation equipment in specified MWR facilities. Policy related to the MWR program is in MCO P1700.27. In matters related to APF support, guidance in the NavCompt Manual governs.

3. Recreation PSE. Equipment used for recreation purposes in BEQ/BOQ common areas or lounges, such as wide screen TV's, pool tables, ping-pong tables, or physical fitness equipment is defined as PSE. Policy for the initial outfitting of recreation equipment in new facilities is in chapter 4 and for replacement equipment in existing facilities in chapter 6 of this Manual.

4. Exclusions. Equipment such as musical instruments, stereo sets, and photographic equipment used for recreation purposes is procured exclusively with NAF.

5. Accountability. All property and equipment procured with appropriated funds for MWR purposes are garrison property and shall be accounted for as delineated in chapter 8 of this Manual. The local MWR office shall account for property and equipment procured with NAF funds as directed in MCO P1700.27. The MWR RO may serve as the RO for garrison property in addition to serving as the RO for NAF equipment. Separate property accounts must be kept for equipment procured with appropriated and NAF dollars.

6. Disposal. MWR equipment procured with appropriated funds shall comply with the disposal procedures in chapter 8 of this Manual and MCO 4500.11

5007. OFFICE MACHINES. Office machines are office laborsaving devices including, but not limited to, manual typewriters, electric typewriters, adding and calculating machines, dictating and transcribing machines, and copiers.

1. Applicability. The policy and procedures of this section comply with FPMR and apply to office machines purchased with both appropriated and nonappropriated funds.

2. References. General inventory control of office machines is maintained per the current procedures governing plant and minor property accounting in the NavCompt Manual, volume 3 and chapters 6 and 8 of this Manual. Policy regarding the acquisition, use, maintenance, and replacement of office machines is in FPMR. Budget guidance for the purchase of office machines is delineated in chapter 6 of this Manual.

3. Data Processing Equipment. General purpose automated data processing equipment and software included in the GSA Supply Catalog FSS FSC Group 70, part I A.

4. Filing Equipment. Filing equipment includes correspondence filing cabinets, mechanized filing, document storage and retrieval systems equipment, and security containers. See MCO 5210.11.

5. Microform System Equipment. See MCO 5210.11 and MCO 5210.13.

6. Electric Typewriters. Acquisition of typewriters must reflect the work of the office. Assign typewriters only to establish positions for which a job or billet description includes a typing or typing function (i.e., multi-pitch) requirement. Limit acquisition of typewriters to standard-type bar, single-pitch machines or single-element machines. Provide each typing station with the lowest cost typewriter to meet the minimum need.

a. Allocation Criteria. When determining requirements for optical character recognition (OCR) capability for non-FMF organizations, use the following criteria.

(1) Disbursing Offices. One typewriter for each person maintaining pay accounts and, if applicable, one typewriter for each allotment, control, or transmittal clerk.

(2) Personnel Offices. One typewriter for each person maintaining service records, processing receipts, and transfers.

(3) Administrative Offices. One typewriter for each administrative and legal clerk responsible to prepare OCR documents.

(4) Housing Offices. One typewriter for each person responsible to prepare OCR documents.

(5) Communications. One typewriter for each office that originates messages through the telecommunications system.

(6) Non typing Personnel. Obsolescent, but usable, typewriters for intermittent use.

b. Special Features. Typewriters with specialized, elaborate, or sophisticated features shall be provided only if the specialized typewriter is the lowest priced typewriter with or without those features, or the features are indispensable to perform the work. Typewriters with special features should not be considered economical unless a high percentage of the work necessitates first-time original copies.

(1) Use of Features. Special features on typewriters and the daily minimum percent of use include but are not limited to the following:

FEATURE	PERCENT
Decimal tab keys or statistical keyboard	55
Multiple-pitch capability	45
Proportional spacing	45

(2) Justification. Acquisition of typewriters with special features required for unique functions shall be justified in writing. The activity commander will approve the acquisition, and the justification shall be made a part of the purchase file.

(3) Type A Font. Type A font OCR typewriters are authorized within the FMF organization. OCR typewriters are for documents used to support the Joint Military Pay System (JUMPS), the Manpower Management System (MMS), and communications applications.

(4) Pooling. When typewriters with specialized features are used only occasionally, they should be pooled within the activity.

(5) Substitution. Activities are authorized to loan electric typewriters to FMF units in garrison as a substitute for manual typewriters.

7. Figuring Machines. Figuring machines include adding machines and calculators (manually or electrically operated), and listing or non listing (excluding the electronic type). They do not include posting or accounting machines.

a. Electric Current. Manual machines should be used where electric current is not conveniently available, where portability is required, where reasonable protection is desired against emergency shutdown, or where a limited requirement does not warrant electric machines.

b. Printed Results. Listing machines shall be used if printed results are necessary to the operation.

c. Work Volume. Figuring machines shall be used if the operation performed contains such a volume of work that is impractical to use slide rules or computation tables.

8. Electronic Office Machines. Electronic office machines are machines having electronic components. Electronic office machines include calculators (programmable and non programmable; portable and desk top; printing, display, and combination print/display types); accounting machines (electronic programmable and nonwriting/numeric; writing/alphanumeric); and cash registers (electronic terminals).

a. Electric Current. Battery-operated machines shall be used where electronic current is not conveniently available, where portability is required, where reasonable protection is desired against emergency shutdown, or where limited use does not warrant electric machines.

b. Printed Results. Electronic listing machines (adding and calculators) shall be used if printed results are necessary to the operation.

c. Work Accuracy. Electronic calculators shall be used if the accuracy or complexity of computations is impractical to expeditiously accomplish by means of slide rules, computation tables, and figuring machines.

9. Printing and Reprographics Equipment

a. Control. The Joint Committee on Printing, Congress of the United States, has established the procedures for reports control and authorization of printing equipment. All printing and reprographics equipment, as defined and classified in MCO P5600.31, are subject to the approval of the CMC (ARE).

b. Authority. Before acquiring printing and reprographics equipment through purchase, rental, exchange, or transfer and before disposal, approval shall be obtained and shall be included with the procurement or disposition documentation. Funds shall not be requested or used unless this authority has been obtained.

10. Procurement of Office Machines. Purchase office equipment on an as-required basis using O&M or PMC funds, as appropriate.

a. Storage. Do not stock office machines and office machine parts in the supply system under any echelon level for procurement.

b. Isolated Locations. When items authorized for local procurement are not available locally, organizations in isolated areas shall forward requests to their normal source of supply for purchase. These requisitions shall cite local funds or Headquarters Marine Corps-held funds when specifically authorized by the CMC and shall contain a statement that the items are not available locally.

c. Forms. The activity Property Control Office shall submit requisitions to GSA on DoD Single Line Item Requisition System Document (Manual) (DD Form 1348) or (Mechanical) (DD Form 1348M) for items listed in the GSA supply catalog. Submit requests for items on FSS to the activity purchasing office.

11. Maintenance for Office Machines. Use instructions in MCO 4860.3 to establish additional maintenance or overhaul facilities for office machines. When such facilities are established, the activity establishing the facility shall report the establishment to the appropriate GSA regional office.

5008. PHYSICAL SECURITY EQUIPMENT. PHSE is intrusion detection systems, access control, assessment and/or closed circuit television systems and equipment, communications systems, and other plant equipment specifically designed for physical security. PHSE is classified as personal property, as opposed to built-in equipment, for budgeting and funding purposes.

1. Authority. Plans to install PHSE must be coordinated with the activity provost marshal and security officer and must comply with the physical security requirements in OPNAV 5530.15. PHSE centrally procured through CMC (POS) shall not be added to, or altered without prior CMC (POS) approval.

2. Initial Outfitting. PHSE systems will be funded as collateral equipment in new facilities under construction. The appropriate military construction appropriation will fund the installation of the new PHSE. Activities will submit to CMC (POS), with a copy to CMC (LFS), PHSE requirements for MCON CE projects. CMC (POS) will validate and approve PHSE requirements for the MILCON, UMC, and GOJ projects. CMC (POS) will forward to Naval Electronics Command at Charleston electronic security system requirements, for validation, prior to return of approved PHSE projects to CMC (LFS).

3. Existing Facility. Installation of PHSE in existing property shall be charged to O&M funds except in the case of a "turnkey installation," when the cost of both equipment, which meets the acquisition criteria, and the installation shall be funded with PMC dollars as an investment cost.

5009. THE OFFICIAL BRONZE MARINE CORPS SEAL AND EMBLEM

1. Marine Corps Seal. Presidential Executive Order 10538 of 22 June 1954 established the basic design for the official seal of the United States Marine Corps. The Secretary of the Navy officially promulgated and adopted the seal for the Marine Corps as described in SECNAVINST 5030.4. The symbolic significance and inherent dignity of the official Marine Corps seal require complete uniformity in its design, coloration, and reproduction for official use.

2. Marine Corps Emblem. The Marine Corps emblem is an eagle, globe, and anchor centered on the Marine Corps seal, without inscription. It was adopted as the official Marine Corps emblem coincident with the approval of the seal by the President.

3. Use of Seal and Emblem. MCO 5030.3 provides specific guidelines for the use of the official Marine Corps seal, emblem, names, or initials. Nongovernment individuals or organizations are authorized use of the emblem under circumstances thal shall reflect favorably upon the Marine Corps or its personnel and that shall conform to the dictates of good taste and propriety. Obtain permission for unofficial use of the emblem and seal from CMC (AR).

4. Responsibility. The CMC (LFS) is charged with the responsibility to determine what uses of the bronze replicas of the seal and emblem constitute "good taste and propriety." The CMC (LFS) shall notify any requester of approval for procurement and shall dictate the source of casting. The private user shall order the bronze emblem directly from the contractor designated by the Marine Corps.

5. Bronze Replica of the Marine Corps Seal. Replicas of the official Marine Corps seal cast in bronze, 15 inches in diameter may be requested for procurement through the CMC (LFS) for use as entrance markers on main gates and official administration buildings at Marine Corps installations. The bronze replica also may be used at military service monuments, which are erected and dedicated on a military installation.

a. Request. Submit requests to the CMC (LFS), indicating funds have been reserved and providing complete justification including the proposed building and location. Bronze replicas are non-stocked items, manufactured individually for direct shipment to the requesting organization.

b. Disposition. Upon disestablishment of an activity or whenever a seal is excess to the needs of the activity, the command should request disposition instructions from CMC (LFS). Bronze replicas of the Marine Corps seal shall not be sold or given to private individuals or organizations.

6. Bronze Replica of the Marine Corps Emblem. Replicas of the official Marine Corps emblem cast in bronze, 15 inches in diameter, may be requested for procurement through the CMC (LFS) for use as markers on main gates such as nonmilitary cemeteries and on nonmilitary dedicated monuments to the military service. The bronze emblem may also be approved for use under circumstances that shall reflect favorably on the Marine Corps or its personnel and shall conform to good taste and propriety.

a. Requests. Requests from non-Marine Corps activities or individuals shall be addressed to the CMC (LFS).

b. Approval. Upon approval for the specific use of the bronze replica, the CMC (LFS) will authorize purchasers to place an order directly with the specified manufacturer, and will authorize the manufacturer to honor the purchase order.

5010. TRAINING AND AUDIOVISUAL EQUIPMENT. Training and audiovisual information support centers (TAVSC) have been organized within the Marine Corps to provide a variety of services, including procurement, loan, and maintenance of training devices, visual information (graphic, photographic, and audio), motion picture equipment, television equipment, and related products.

1. Reference. Policy related to the Marine Corps Training and Audiovisual Support program is in MCO P5290.1.

2. Initial Outfitting. Requirements for TAVIS equipment for new facilities should be submitted to CMC (LFS), through the local comptroller or fiscal office, as delineated in chapter 4 of this Manual. A duplicate copy of the MCON CE list shall be furnished to CG MCCDC (TE35) Quantico for inclusion in the TAVIS program budgets.

3. Loans. A deploying unit may be authorized to take audiovisual products and training devices accounted for as garrison property if there is a valid reason and if the activity TAVSC can afford to loan the equipment. The decision to loan the equipment can be made at the activity level for the period of deployment. Additional policy related to temporary loans is delineated in chapter 8 of this Manual.

4. Property Management. TAVIS equipment is managed, Controlled, and accounted for under the procedures delineated in chapter 8 of this Manual. CG MCCD (TE35) Quantico will manage TAVIS equipment inventories and provide instructions for TAVIS equipment transfer disposal.

5011. UNINTERRUPTED POWER SUPPLY (UPS). UPS refers to the uninterrupted power supply or no break power units installed to provide uninterrupted service of near-perfect voltage and predetermined cycles as protection against power outages from the normal source of electrical power.

1. Personal Property. UPS installed and used for the integral support of other equipment, such as communications, electronic, cryptographic, or computer equipment is classified as personal property. UPS defined as personal or garrison property is managed and funded as directed in this Manual.

2. Installed Equipment. UPS intended to serve a facility or provide power to a building as a whole is classified as installed equipment. The initial costs for installed UPS are defined as construction costs. UPS defined as installed equipment is managed and funded as directed in MCO P11000.5.

5012. WAREHOUSE EQUIPMENT. Warehouse equipment includes automated material handling systems, storage systems and support equipment, and preservation, packaging, and packing systems. Typical equipment includes conveyors, wrapping machines, carton closure equipment, and shelving systems. Wheeled, motorized material handling equipment, such as pallet trucks, forklifts, stock selectors, and scooters, is managed and controlled separately under the GME programs.

1. Reference. Policy related to Marine Corps warehousing is in MCO P4450.7. Additional policy for warehouse operations and modernization planning is in MCO P4450.10 and in NAVSUP PUB529.

2. Classification. Warehouse equipment is classified as class 3 or 4 plant property or minor property, dependent on the acquisition criteria specified in chapter 6 of this Manual.

3. Accountability. Warehouse equipment used at Marine Corps facilities is accounted for as garrison property. FMF units assigned warehouse equipment for operations in field warehouses shall comply with policy in MCO P4450.7 and MCO P4400.150.

4. Initial Outfitting. Warehouse equipment is provided as MCON CE for new warehouse facilities. Activities should complete the project documentation delineated in chapter 4 of this Manual. Contact the base warehouse officer for assistance to determine the appropriate items for each application.

5. Replacement Equipment. Normal replacement of obsolete or unserviceable warehouse equipment is budgeted for as directed in chapter 6 of this Manual.

6. Warehouse Modernization (Whose Mod). Plans for Whse Mod should include equipment requirements to accomplish the total modernization of the warehouse facility. Activities submit Whse Mod project requirements, annually for the budget year and 5 additional years, to CMC (LFS) as directed in MCO P4450.10.

7. Warehouse Systems. The acquisition of warehouse systems for automated handling storage equipment shall comply with the expense and investment criteria delineated in chapter 6 of this Manual.

CHAPTER 6

BUDGETING

CHAPTER 6

BUDGETING

6000. GENERAL INFORMATION. This chapter addresses the policy and procedures used to budget for garrison property. Budgets are used to plan, program, allocate, and execute the resources used to operate Marine Corps activities. Two important elements of the budget preparation and administration process within the Marine Corps are budget formulation and budget execution. The method used in the formulation process is referred to as the planning, programming, and budgeting system (PPBS).

6001. REFERENCE. Policy on the budget process is in the NavCompt Manual, volume 7, MCO P7100.8, and a MCO in the 3121 series.

6002. RESPONSIBILITY. Budget submissions for garrison property requirements shall be coordinated through the comptroller or fiscal office at each activity. FMF or tenant activities shall identify requirements to acquire, maintain, or support garrison property to the host activity for inclusion in the activity or supporting establishment budget.

6003. OVERVIEW OF PLANT AND MINOR PROPERTY

1. Personal Capital Plant Equipment. Personal capital plant equipment is Government-owned nonexpendable equipment having an initial unit cost of $5,000 or more, acquired or issued to produce supplies or perform services, or for any administrative or general plant support purposes to further the assigned mission of an activity. Command support equipment (CSE) is known interchangeably as plant property, base property, station property, or garrison property. Among specific equipment excluded are items in the possession of tactical forces and items that are part of the stock fund appropriation. Specific categories of plant property not included in the CSE program are in the NavCompt Manual, paragraph 036301.4.

a. Class 3 Plant Property. Class 3 plant property includes all Marine Corps-owned personal property of a capital nature with an estimated or actual initial cost of $5,000 or more. It must meet all criteria in the NavCompt Manual, paragraph 036301.2. Equipment specifically excluded from reporting as class 3 property is listed in the NavCompt Manual, paragraph 036301.4.

b. Class 4 Plant Property Industrial Plant Equipment (IPE)

(1) Class 4 plant property is all equipment with an acquisition cost of $5,000 in Federal Supply Group 34 used to cut, abrade, grind, shape, form, join, test, measure, heat, treat, or otherwise alter the physical, electrical, or chemical properties of materials, components, or end items used in manufacturing, maintenance, supply, processing, assembly, or research and development operations. Class 4 property is under Defense Industrial Plant Equipment Center (DIPEC) cognizance. Equipment specifically excluded from reporting as class 4 plant property is in the NavCompt Manual, paragraph 036401.2.

(2) As provided in the NavCompt Manual, paragraph 036003, the Director, Naval Industrial Resources Support Activity (NAVIRSA), Philadelphia, Pennsylvania, via the Chief of Naval Operations (OP-46) and Defense Finance and Accounting Service, Washington Center (DFAS) shall provide to the CMC (LFS) all Navy implementing policy and procedures related to uniform acquisition and management of the IPE program. The Director, NAVIRSA, shall conduct on-site assistance visits at major activities within available resources.

The NAVIRSA shall perform on-site reviews of the Marine Corps implementation of Navy-owned property management directives, prepare reports of deficiencies, and recommend corrective action.

2. Minor Property. In the NavCompt Manual, paragraph 036701, minor property is defined as personal property acquired for immediate use with a unit cost less than $5,000 which does not meet plant property acquisition criteria. O&MMC funds are used to procure minor property. Sample minor property items are listed in appendix K. The data base for minor property accountability will include, at a minimum, all property costing $300 to less than $5,000, specifically including furniture, fixtures, office or industrial equipment, equipment classified or sensitive less than $5,000, and all pilferable items costing $100 but less than $5,000.

6004. ACQUISITION CRITERIA. The funding responsibilities for appropriations and accounts in Department of Navy acquisition are in the NavCompt Manual, volume 7. Expense and investment criteria determine the appropriation used to finance equipment acquisition.

1. Expense Property. Expense items are those items with a unit value less than $15,000 financed through the O&MMC or O&MMCR appropriations. This type property is not designated for centralized item management by an item manager or included in the Marine Corps stores account. Expense items are procured with O&MMC funds provided in the operating budget available at the local level or provided from CMC directed programs. Expense property will be accounted for as plant or minor property, dependent on the acquisition cost.

2. Investment Property. Investment items are those capital assets with a unit cost of $15,000 or more financed through the PMC appropriation. Equipment stocked in the Marine Corps stores account or similar type allowance equipment in the possession of tactical forces is excluded. A current certificate of nonavailability (CNA) is required before procurement of class 4 equipment is initiated, as indicated in chapter 7 of this Manual.

6005. BUDGETING: INVESTMENT (PLANT) PROPERTY

1. Investment Property. CSE is class 3 and 4 investment plant property with a unit cost of $15,000 or more used at Marine Corps activities to support the operations and mission of the host and tenant activities.

a. Class 3. Budget categories of class 3 property, and major items within the categories are as follows (similar equipment may be expense property dependent on the cost):

(1) Buildings and Grounds. This group includes cranes (stationary), floor sanders, floor scrubbers, vacuum cleaners, waste compactors, and attachments or auxiliary equipment to end items such as mowers, plows, road sweepers, and sprayers.

(2) Office Equipment. This group includes accounting and calculating machines, addressing machines, bookbinding equipment, cash registers, dictating and transcribing machines, duplicating equipment, printing equipment, safes, time recorders, typewriters, copiers, and visible record equipment.

(3) Utilities Equipment. This group includes battery chargers, compressors, engine generators, fire extinguishers, intercoms, public address systems, radar speed equipment, radio sets, rectifiers, facsimile machines, telephone equipment, and teletypewriters.

(4) General Purpose Equipment. This group includes boats, bonding machines, conveyors, hand trucks, hoists, musical instruments, packaging and wrapping machinery, safety equipment, security equipment, sound modules, audiovisual support equipment, and laundry equipment. Laundry equipment includes air

forms, automatic shirt/coat units, conveyors, cross folders, feed spreaders, flat ironers, marking machines, spotting boards, stackers/counters, steam presses, steam tunnels, stills, synthetic solvent cleaning units, tumblers, utility presses, and washers/extractors.

(5) Environmental Equipment. This group is used to support compliance with environmental protection programs. Includes such items as recycling, tire shredding, pollution abatement, underground storage testing, environmental medium testing (air, soil, and water), and environmental processing equipment. GME in support of these programs such as forklifts or vehicles are not included in the CSE budget. Identify these items separately in the GME budget.

(6) Food Services Equipment. This group includes refrigerators, freezers, dishwashers, drinking water coolers, waste disposal systems, hoods, and vents used in food service operations.

b. Class 4. IPE includes such equipment as drills, furnaces, grinders, lathes, miscellaneous maintenance and repair shop specialized equipment, scales, shapers, forging machines, optical instruments, rolling mills, non-TAM saws, weatherometers, and welders.

2. Expense Plant Property. Class 3 expense plant property is equipment with a unit cost of $5,000 but less than $15,000 used at Marine Corps activities to support the operations and mission of the host and tenant activities. O&MMC funds are used to procure this plant property.

3. Restricted Garrison Property. The following list, although not all-inclusive, contains exceptions to the general rule of garrison property items, due to restrictions established by higher authority or because certain items are purchased from funds not available to the local commanders. Where applicable, current directives provide guidance for activity commanders to submit budget requirements.

a. Air-Conditioning Equipment. Budget submissions for air-conditioning equipment shall comply with MCO P11000.9.

b. Test, Measurement, and Diagnostic Equipment. Budget submissions for test, measurement, and diagnostic equipment shall comply with MCO P4733.1.

c. Clubs Equipment. Budget submissions for Marine Corps clubs equipment shall comply with MCO P1700.27.

d. ADPE. Budget submissions for both expense and investment ADPE shall comply with MCO P5230.15.

e. Electronic Test and Measuring Equipment. Budget submissions for electronic test and measuring equipment shall comply with MCO 10510.18.

f. Filing Equipment. Budget submissions for filing equipment shall comply with MCO 5210.11. Procurement of legal size or oversize filing equipment is restricted to mission critical requirements, supported with justification to CMC (ARDB).

g. Family Housing. Budget submissions for furniture, furnishings, and equipment for family housing shall comply with MCO P11000.22.

h. GME. Budget submissions for GME, including engineering equipment, materials handling equipment, and vehicles shall comply with MCO P11240.106.

i. Laundry and Dry-Cleaning Equipment. Budget submissions for laundry and dry-cleaning equipment shall comply with MCO P4064.3.

j. Microfilming (Microform) Equipment. Budget submissions for microfilming (microform) equipment shall comply with MCO 5210.11 and MCO 5210.13.

k. Mobile Electric Power (Generators). Budget submissions for mobile electric power (generators) shall comply with MCO 11310.10.

l. Musical Instruments. Budget submissions for musical instruments shall comply with MCO 4225.2

m. MWR Equipment. Budget submissions for MWR equipment shall comply with MCO P1700.27, SECNAVINST 7000.23, and NavCompt Manual, volume 7.

n. Training and Audiovisual Support Equipment. Budget submissions shall comply with MCO P5290.1.

o. Printing/Duplicating/Copying Equipment. Before procurement and regardless of unit cost, printing, duplicating, and copying equipment must have the CMC (ARE) approval to comply with MCO P5600.31.

p. Relocatable Buildings. Requirements for relocatable buildings are in chapter 5 of this Manual and MCO P11000.12.

q. Warehouse Modernization Equipment. Budget submissions for warehouse modernization equipment shall comply with MCO 4450.10.

r. Medical and Dental Equipment. Before procurement of all medical and dental equipment, technical "approval for use" from the Bureau of Medicine and Surgery is required to comply with NavCompt Manual, paragraph 035132 and BUMEDINST 6700.16.

4. Budget Formulation - CSE

a. Steps. The activity budget plan for plant property includes the following steps:

(1) Identify and validate activity plant property requirements. Use the format in appendix L.

(2) Submit CSE aggregate budget category totals to CMC (LFS) through the activity comptroller before 30 November each year. Use the format in appendix L.

(3) Submit prioritized unfunded requirements for the next budget year and from previous years to CMC (LFS) as an attachment to the third quarter CSE status report (RCS DN-7301-04) due 10 July each year. This submit becomes the basis for funds allocation for the next budget year. Use the format in appendix L. This report is exempt from reports control.

b. Requirements Identification. Activity commanders shall develop the plant property requirements budget to comply with the following guidelines:

(1) Replacement. Determine if the equipment forecasted for replacement on the plant account listing should be replaced within the planned budget cycle. If not, update account records to correct replacement year and condition code.

(2) Maintenance Improvement. Determine if equipment with recurring maintenance problems should be replaced. Recurring maintenance costs and newer technology may indicate continued operation is not cost-effective.

(3) New Technology. Determine if new technology is available to generate productivity, efficiency, and laborsavings.

(4) Budget Justification. Seek necessary approvals to comply with guidance issued from higher management (see paragraph 6005.3), or established at the local level, develop specifications for each requirement identified, and prepare a logistics plan for the procurement documentation (PD).

(5) Cost. Transportation and installation costs of equipment shall be included in the total item cost. The procurement and installation of installed equipment are construction costs and shall be funded from the available construction appropriation. Installation of garrison or personal property shall be funded with the same appropriation used to procure the equipment. Activities shall include installation in the terms of the contract, to the extent possible, for the supplier (contractor) to accomplish the equipment installation. The total item cost distinction applies even if the dealer's invoice shows these charges as separate items. The NavCompt Manual, paragraph 036203.15, applies.

(6) Economic Analysis. Complete an economic analysis as delineated in chapter 7 of this Manual for all equipment scheduled for commercial procurement. The economic analysis shall be retained with the activity comptroller as backup.

c. Aggregate Budget. Activities shall submit an aggregate CSE budget for each equipment category (see paragraph 6005.1) for review and evaluation. The budget is due to CMC (LFS) each 30 November for the current year and the next 3 successive budget years. Submit each category separately on the format entitled "Command Support Equipment (CSE) Budget Requirements," shown in appendix L. The outyear budget requirements are reviewed and the requirements consolidated for planning purposes in the program objective memorandum (POM) process.

d. Requirements Prioritization. Activities shall submit to CMC (LFS) a prioritized list of any validated, unfunded, prior year requirements and all approved new requirements for current year funding. Activities submit these requirements in the third quarter status report, along with the status of current and prior year funds. This prioritized list in effect becomes the basis for funding from the current year appropriation.

5. Funds Authorization

a. Allocation. Available funds will be allocated to activities each year after the funds are authorized to the CMC Fiscal Director (FD). Initiate procurement action to commit funds immediately for all items on the prioritized list, within the funds authorized. The activity comptroller has the authority to reprogram authorized funds to satisfy reprioritized requirements. Indicate such changes on the next quarterly status report.

b. Obligation. Obligate funds within the amount allocated for the appropriation. If additional funds are required to complete a procurement action, the activity through the local comptroller or fiscal office shall request the additional amount from the CMC program sponsor before obligation is made. Report excess funds promptly after all requirements have been obligated.

(1) Procurement Initiative. Once a requirement has been budgeted, activities should initiate action for all required PD up to funds commitment to expedite contract obligation after the activity receives the funds. Activities should plan to fully commit funds immediately on receipt of authorization document (NavCompt Form 372).

(2) Contract Obligation. Obligate funds authorized to procure investment items within 60 days after receipt of the authorization document (NavCompt Form 372). While the CSE PMC program is a 3-year appropriation, activities shall make every effort for 100 percent obligation within the first year of authorization.

c. Status. Activities shall forward a budget status report to the CMC (LFS) for all current and prior year funds in the format entitled "Command Support Equipment Status Report," shown in appendix L. Update actual cost, priority, and planned obligation date (month and year) each quarter if changes have occurred. Make plans to procure the property during the first year of the appropriation to avoid withdrawal for other programmed requirements.

d. Procurement. Accomplish procurement as directed in chapter 8 of this Manual and through the coordinated procurement program assignee, as appropriate.

6. Appropriation Data. The accounting classification used in appropriation data to procure plant property shall comply with the NavCompt Manual, volume 2. The accounting classification is used with functional accounts. The following specific guidance applies for plant property:

a. Property Accounting Activity (PAA). The PAA is the UIC of the activity responsible to prepare the NavCompt Form 167. Use the PAA when the TT indicates a purchase is a direct charge to the activity plant property account.

b. Transaction Type (TT). The transaction type designator identifies charges to the plant property account. The TT generates a report to notify the plant account officer plant property is on order. Apply these codes at the commitment or obligation level for investment items procured with PMC funds:

1H Plant property account code for formal departmental obligations. The code includes items costing $5,000 or more, but is not applicable for use with O&MMC funds. Excludes items for delivery to contractors.

1I Plant property account code for direct procurement of items costing $5,000 or more. The code is not for formal departmental obligations but is not applicable for use with O&MMC funds. Excludes items for delivery to contractors.

A TT code is not designated for expense items with a cost between $5,000 - $15,000 and procured with O&MMC funds.

c. Abstract of Public Vouchers. On the summary register, code 4c identifies plant property. The TT defined in paragraph 6005.6b, of this Manual, will appear on the daily abstract report. Use the TT entry for plant property on the daily register or summary reports to reconcile work-in-progress related to class 3 or 4 plant property purchases ant to make adjustments on the NavCompt Form 167 discussed in chapter 8 of this Manual.

6006. BUDGETING: EXPENSE PROPERTY

1. Expense Property. For budgeting purposes, plant property with a unit cost of $5,000 to $15,000 and minor property with a unit value less than $5,000 are defined as expense items, financed through the O&MMC or O&MMCR appropriations.

2. PSE Budget. Conduct the physical inventory for the PSE Annual Inventory Report (RCS DN-7110-03), shown in appendix L,during the period from 1 July to 15 August each year to determine local PSE requirements.

a. Budget. PSE requirements identified for replacement, augmentation, or refurbishment constitute the PSE budget. Use the format entitled "Personnel Support Equipment (PSE) Annual Inventory Report," shown in appendix L, to submit the consolidated activity requirements to CMC (LFS) before 15 September each year. Chapter 8 of this Manual provides guidelines for the inventory process.

b. Funds. Funds provided for PSE property will be identified as an addition to the activity budget base, as a separate line item in the activity operating budget (OPBUD) at the start of the fiscal year.

c. Policy. Chapter 2 of this Manual provides additional guidance about the PSE program.

3. FPSE Budget. FPSE requirements that meet the investment criteria shall be identified for PMC funding using the procedures in paragraph 6005. Food service officers shall identify FPSE requirements which meet the expense criteria, including plant property equipment acquired with O&MMC funds.

a. Budget. The comptroller at each activity shall submit the validated FPSE expense requirements to CMC (LFS) before 31 January each year, for each budget year (BY and BY +1) using the format discussed in chapter 3 of this Manual and shown in appendix L. This report is exempt from reports control. Comptroller review provides for independent review of the FPSE budget. Funding for consumable items such as paper products, linens, cutlery, dishes, and silverware is the responsibility of the local activity.

b. Funds. Funds for FPSE property, other than investment items, will be identified as a separate line item in the activity OPBUD at the start of the fiscal year.

c. Installation. Costs to install expense equipment shall not be included in the FPSE O&MMC budget. Installation costs for budget items shall be included in the OPBUD requirements at the activity level. Costs to install and transport investment equipment shall be included in the item cost. Installation shall be funded from the same appropriation used to procure the equipment. When installation is specified in the contract, installation costs shall be included in the project for the equipment, whether Government-furnished and contractor-installed, or contractor-furnished and contractor-installed on a turnkey basis. Installation costs for expense FPSE in MFIP projects shall be included with the other equipment costs for the project.

d. Policy. Chapter 3 of this Manual provides additional guidance about the FPSE program.

4. MCON CE. Submit requirements for the initial outfitting of new or renovated facilities as delineated in chapter 4 of this Manual. Requirements submitted for MILCON projects shall be excluded from other budget submissions.

5. ADPE. Budget for ADPE/WPE/OISE as delineated in chapter 5 section 4 of MCO P7100.8K. Peripheral equipment to support ADPE shall be budgeted for as CSE (plant property) or minor property, dependent on the acquisition criteria in paragraph 6004 of this Manual.

6. Other Minor Property. Minor property, acquired for immediate use with local O&M funds, is authorized on an "as required" basis to support activities and FMF tenants in a garrison environment.

a. Policy. The minor property budget shall include requirements to replace obsolete or worn out equipment and equipment for technology or productivity improvements. Base operations support is provided for administrative and buildings and grounds functions. Chapter 5 of this Manual provides additional guidance about minor property.

b. Budget. Appendix K provides a list, although not all-inclusive, of typical minor property items. Identify minor property requirements using the format entitled "Minor Property Requirements," shown in appendix L. Identify deficiencies above the activity ceiling in part A. Show the total requirements in part B. The difference between part B and part A is the activity ceiling for minor property.

c. Maintenance. Costs to maintain garrison property shall be included in the minor property budget. Funds can be used for repair and maintenance costs either through in-house maintenance or maintenance contacts.

d. Exclusions. For budget purposes, minor property does not include PSE, FPSE, MCON CE, ADPE, or equipment funded under other O&MMC programs. The budget process for these programs is discussed elsewhere in this chapter.

7. Turnkey Projects. A turnkey project exists when a contract specifies the contractor provides all equipment, installation, improvement, repair, and construction for the project. Several appropriations may be combined to obligate the contract. A typical example is an MFIP project that requires PMC funds for the investment equipment, FPSE O&MMC for expense equipment, and repair O&MMC funds for the minor construction.

a. Investment Property. When the equipment for the project meets the investment criteria and represents the major portion of the total project cost, the project cost shall be included in the plant equipment budget, regardless of approval authority.

b. Type Projects. Turnkey projects funded under the PMC appropriation shall be limited to the procurement and installation of a major equipment item, a complete operating system, a complete shop, or a complete facility.

c. CMC Approval. Projects for facility repair and/or construction that exceed the local activity commander's approval authority shall comply with MCO P11000.5. Forward such projects to CMC (LFF) for approval.

d. Installation Costs. Installations shall be funded from the same appropriation used to procure the equipment. When installation is specified in the contract, installation costs shall be included in the project for the equipment, whether Government-furnished and contractor-installed or contractor-furnished and contractor-installed on a turnkey basis.

GARRISON PROPERTY POLICY MANUAL

CHAPTER 7

PROPERTY ACQUISITION

GARRISON PROPERTY POLICY MANUAL

CHAPTER 7

PROPERTY ACQUISITION

7000. GENERAL INFORMATION. Procurement refers to the contractual process of gaining possession of property. This chapter addresses screening, sources of supply, priorities of sources, and other acquisition considerations.

1. Reference. Acquisition of garrison property shall comply with the FAR and MCO P4200.15 and shall be effected through the coordinated procurement program assignee, when appropriate.

2. Equipment Allowances. Plant property items, not controlled by allowance documents, are authorized on an as-required basis, except for those items listed in paragraph 6005.3 of this Manual. Those items are excepted because of restrictions established from a higher authority level or because the items are purchased from funds not available to the local commander.

3. DoD System Requisitions. Garrison property items shall not be requisitioned from the MCLB, Albany, even though the equipment may appear in current management data lists.

4. IPE. DoD policy is that usable IPE shall be reutilized to the maximum extent possible to preclude duplicate investment. The DIPEC is responsible to control DoD IPE. NavCompt Manual, paragraph 036403, contains guidance for acquiring class 4 IPE.

7001. PROCUREMENT CONSIDERATIONS

1. Economic Analysis. Complete an economic analysis for all garrison property scheduled for commercial procurement. The computer adaptable format shown in appendix L can be used for most buys. This analysis shall not be submitted in the budget but shall be included with the procurement documentation and made available to CMC staff offices when requested. MCO 7000.12 provides guidance.

2. Feasibility. Before acquisition of the equipment specified in this Manual, consider the following:

a. Length of time the equipment will be used, including extent of use.

b. Financial and other advantages of all types and makes of equipment available.

c. Comparison of lease costs and purchase costs.

d. Cost of purchase and installation.

e. Imminent technological improvements.

f. Other pertinent factors.

3. Maximum Use. All activities shall make maximum use of property to minimize requests for replacement or purchase of new equipment. Before procurement, commands shall fill needs insofar as practicable through redistribution, repair, or rehabilitation of property on hand.

4. Phase-In. Activities should have a systematic means of phasing in new property, for example, place newly acquired property in functions with high use and move older serviceable items into functions having low use.

7002. PROPERTY SELECTION

1. Essential Nature. Limit procurement of new items to those essential to improve productivity or efficiency, to optimize use of space, and to enhance living or working conditions. Quality of life enhancements to the appearance, decor, or status shall be made only in conjunction with essential requirements, but shall not be accomplished to satisfy the desire for the latest design or more expensive lines of property. Garrison property must be selected considering durability, comfort, interchangeability, and safety required for the use the item will receive.

2. Economic Considerations. Consolidate requirements to optimize the benefits and lower prices obtainable through definite quantity or larger volume procurements. The quantity, quality, and variety of property should be limited to that required to adequately perform the function. To the extent practicable, activities should standardize the types, sizes, colors, and designs of property procured to facilitate interchange, maintenance, repair, and replacement.

3. Approval. The activity commander or his designee shall approve the procurement of garrison property from any source. Limit procurement to the least expensive lines which meet the operational and/or support requirement, yet meet quality standards to ensure durability and standardization.

4. Priority of Sources. Activities shall satisfy requirements through the following sources listed in order of precedence:

a. Activity inventory.

b. Excess from other activities.

c. Federal Prison Industries.

d. Procurement lists of products available from the Committee for Purchase from the Blind and Other Severely Handicapped.

e. GSA stock program.

f. Mandatory FSS's.

g. Optional use FSS's.

h. Commercial sources.

7003. SCREENING

1. Excess Listings. Review excess lists from other activities, from DoD components, and from other agencies for serviceable and acceptable property to satisfy requirements. The review of DoD and GSA excess lists for possible use of items listed therein, before initiating procurement actions, is directed in MCO 4500.11.

2. Defense Reutilization and Marketing Office (DRMO). Activities are responsible to screen DRMO for excess property. The Defense Utilization Program is one of the first sources of supply for all DoD components. The Defense Logistics Agency (DLA) is administrator of the program within DoD. The DLA operates several systems designed to make DoD components aware of available excess property, its location,

and its physical condition. These systems range from the mechanized front end screening system, which involves the wholesale level, to manual systems such as weekly excess personal property lists and high-dollar value flyers.

3. Asset Information. The Defense Reutilization and Marketing Service (DRMS), a field command of DLA located at Battle Creek, Michigan, can provide asset data upon request through dial-up or direct on-line access. The Integrated Disposal Management System described in MCO 4500.11 provides asset availability information, generally on a 24-hour response basis. A requiring activity may institute interrogations for excess assets either on a one-time basis or for a specified period under the "want list" concept. When the interrogation confirms that assets located in DRMO channels meet the established requirements, the requiring activity is advised by telephone, message, or letter of the location, condition, and other relevant data.

4. Certificate of Nonavailability (CNA). As directed in NavCompt Manual and DLAM 4215.1, activities must screen DIPEC before purchasing class 4 IPE with an acquisition cost of $15,000 or more. A current CNA must be submitted to the contracting office before procurement of class 4 IPE is initiated. The CNA expires after 90 days if procurement action has not commenced. Direct screening with DIPEC is possible through the DLA General Reserve Interrogation Program (GRIP) at Memphis, Tennessee.

5. ADPE. Activities must comply with the mandated screening process in DoD Manual 7950.1-M before acquisition of new ADPE. The listings and screening reports differ from those DRMS, Battle Creek, Michigan, provides.

7004. SOURCE OF SUPPLY

1. Government Sources. Select garrison property, furniture, furnishings, and equipment from the following prioritized Government sources of supply to the maximum extent possible after evaluating price, delivery, and property compatibility requirements:

a. Federal Prison Industries (FPI). FPI is a wholly owned Government corporation which has adopted the trade name UNICOR. FPI offers products both through their mandatory schedule of products and throught their own catalogs of items made in federal corrections institutions. Typical items available through FPI include the military specification for bunk bed and accessories, storage shelving, and several lines of office furniture.

b. Procurement List of Blind and Other Severely Handicapped Products. The procurement list the Committee for Purchase from the Blind and Other Severely Handicapped publishes is a mandatory source of supply.

c. GSA Stores Stock Catalogs

(1) GSA Supply Catalog Series. The GSA Supply Catalog Series is the major merchandising instrument of the stock program. This series is published in five volumes and consists of a guide and four commodity catalogs.

(2) GSA Supply Catalog Guide. The GSA Supply Catalog Guide contains consolidated alphabetic noun names and NSN indexes which may be used to locate items in any of the following four commodity catalogs:

(a) Industrial Products Catalog. The Industrial Products Catalog has limited furnishing items, such as mattress pads and covers, pillow covers, and clocks.

(b) Office Products Catalog. The Office Products Catalog has limited furnishings, such as waste baskets, ash trays, and flag stands.

(c) Furniture Catalog. The Furniture Catalog has been developed as a source for the selection of GSA stock office furniture.

(d) Tools Catalog. The Tools Catalog covers an assortment of small hand tools.

d. FSS's. FSS's issued by GSA cover furnishings, furniture, and equipment which provide the procuring activity with sources of supply for standard commercial items in varying quantities at price discounts associated with volume buying. These published schedules are mandatory to the extent specified in each schedule. Explanation of the schedules; e.g., competitive (single award), multiple award, and new item introduction schedules, is as follows:

(1) FSS Program Guide. The FSS Program Guide explains how to use FSS's.

(2) Property Rehabilitation Service. In addition to the listed schedules for the purchase of new items, the FSS program lists contracts for maintenance, repair, and rehabilitation services issued and administered by FSS regional property rehabilitation branches.

(3) Competitive (Single Award) Schedules. Competitive schedules cover contracts with one supplier at a stated price for delivery to a particular geographical area. These contract items are normally manufactured to a Government specification or standard and are normally awarded on a competitive basis each year.

(4) Multiple Award Schedules. Multiple Award Schedules cover contracts and agreements from manufacturers supplying the same generic item, such as desks, chairs, and conference tables, at varying prices. These contracts are with GSA on a negotiated basis for a specified time (usually 1 year) with several suppliers of comparable items who provide selectivity among items for which there are no prescribed Government specifications or standards.

(5) New Item Introductory Schedule. The New Item Inventory Schedule provides the means to test demand for new or improved items not presently entered in any of GSA's supply systems.

e. GSA Special Buying Program. The maximum order limitation (MOL) is a quantitative ceiling on the FSS. If the contracting/purchasing officer has a large order that exceeds the MOL, the order must be sent to the GSA regional support office serving the agency headquarters for a special buying program called "Definitive Quantity Procurement."

(1) Competitive Schedule. If the MOL is exceeded for an item from a competitive schedule, the Furniture Commodity Center will send out the Government specification and the lowest bidder will be awarded a contract.

(2) Multiple Award. If the MOL is exceeded on an item from a multiple award schedule, the contracting or purchasing officer must provide the Furniture Commodity Center a specification describing the salient features of the item. The Furniture Commodity Center will use this specification to request and evaluate bids, and award a contract to the lowest conforming bidder.

(3) Lead Time. The definitive quantity procurement procedure requires a minimum of 6 months lead time before an award of contract.

f. Department of Defense Supply System. The national supply system is a concept designed to eliminate avoidable duplication of supply functions between GSA, DoD, and other Federal agencies. Normally, garrison property is not requisitioned through the DoD Supply System.

2. Commercial Sources. Purchases from commercial sources in the open market must be held to a minimum and must be fully justified. The preceding Government sources are intended to fulfill most Marine Corps property needs. When an item is not available from a Government source, the requiring activity shall prepare drawings, specifications, and justifications for the item in question so bids may be solicited. Advice and assistance in this area are available from the activity contracting and purchasing office.

a. Sole Source Procurement. When the item desired is not available from a Government source, and only available from one source, follow the requirement of the FAR relating to other than full and open competition. In addition, furnish the following information to the contracting and purchasing officer:

(1) A complete and detailed description of the item.

(2) A copy of the manufacturer's cut and/or specification sheet that shows all pertinent details of the item, such as size, material, furnish manufacturer's standards, test, and approval by agencies such as Underwriters Laboratory.

(3) A detailed justification statement indicating why this item, and this item only, is required, and why it is not possible to obtain competition in its acquisition.

7005. SPECIAL PROVISIONS

1. Waivers to Government Sources. When an activity commander determines that an item available from GSA stock or FSS will not serve the required functional end-use purpose, a request to waive the requirement for use of GSA sources shall be submitted to the GSA via the CMC (LFS).

a. Address. Commissioner
General Services Administration
Federal Supply Service
Washington, DC 20406

b. Description. Descriptive literature such as costs, illustrations, drawings, and brochures which show the characteristics or construction of the item or explain its operation should be furnished whenever possible.

c. Comparison of Price and Technical Differences. List the inadequacies of the GSA item in performing required functions. List advantages of the requested item such as technical, economic, or other qualities. List quantity required. If demand is recurring, estimate annual usage; state if demand is nonrecurring or unpredictable.

2. Alternate Sources. FPMR, DAR, and MCO P4200.15 require ordering activities to purchase supplies and services, which are listed in the mandatory GSA FSS's from the GSA schedule even though a similar item or service might be available from another source at a lower price.

a. Identical Products. When an ordering activity finds an identical product (make and model number) or service is available from noncontract sources at a delivered price lower than the delivered contract price quoted in FSS, the activity may purchase such item or service at the lower price without violating the contract requirements. When activities do purchase identical items at lower prices, the activities shall submit a copy of the purchase document to:

Commissioner
General Services Administration (FSS)
Federal Supply Service
Washington, DC 20406

b. Maintenance of FSS's. Information provided herein is not intended to contravene the FSS program. Purchasing activities shall not solicit bids or proposals or otherwise test the market solely for the purpose of seeking alternative sources to the mandatory FSS's. Activities shall not request formal or informal quotations from FSS contractors for purposes of contract price comparisons. Local activities shall continue to maintain a complete file of FSS as previously required.

3. Certification. Each separate request for procurement action requires that the following certification be signed by the installation commander/authorizing official:

"I certify that the requested item/items are not available from excess or surplus within the local command or geographic location and that procurement action is in full compliance with FPMR, sections 101-25, 101-26.101, 101-43.3, and 105."

4. Substitute Items. Procurement needs placed on GSA will be met through issue from stock at regional facilities or through use of existing GSA contracts. For economy, it is mandatory that substitute items available at Marine Corps supply activities or obtained through the services of GSA for the Marine Corps must be accepted as issued, except when to do so would be in conflict with security regulations.

GARRISON PROPERTY POLICY MANUAL

CHAPTER 8

PROPERTY MANAGEMENT

CHAPTER 8

PROPERTY MANAGEMENT

8000. GENERAL INFORMATION. This chapter addresses the management and control of garrison property through identification, maintenance, replacement, transfer, loan, and disposal.

8001. RESPONSIBILITY

1. Property Administrator. Each owning activity shall designate a minor property administrator responsible to maintain the property management system controlling minor property. The minor property administrator shall maintain a minor property database by the responsible officer (RO).

2. Responsible Officer. An RO is an individual appointed by proper authority to exercise custody, care, and safekeeping for the property entrusted to the possession or under the supervision of that individual. Financial liability may be incurred for losses occurring from the individual's failure to exercise this obligation. RO responsibilities are delineated in MCO P4400.150.

3. Fiscal Officer. Fiscal officers are responsible to establish and maintain the official financial plant property records of assigned activities, to identify and report plant property, and submit financial reports, as well as other assigned duties.

4. Accountability. Accountability is the obligation imposed by law or lawful order or regulation on an individual in authority to keep accurate records of property, documents, or funds. The individual having accountability responsibility may or may not have actual possession of property, documents, or functions. Accountability is concerned primarily with custody, care, and safekeeping. Activity commanders shall designate responsible officers who have responsibility for the garrison property in their possession or under their supervision. Additional provisions for accountability are delineated in MCO P4400.150.

8002. DOCUMENTATION. Marine Corps activities shall account for all Government personal property procured with appropriated funds, regardless of the source, used at the Marine Corps activity.

1. Plant Property

a. Records. Report the acquisition of a plant account item (cost $5,000 or greater) promptly to the plant account office within the accountable plant account activity (PAA) or fiscal office on, but no later than, the 10th calendar day immediately following the quarter the property was physically received. A DoD property record, in the format shown in appendix L, must be prepared for each item. If installation is required, prepare an interim DoD property record. The fiscal office shall include the cost of the item on the first Reconciliation of Plant Account (NavCompt Form 167) after receipt of the record. Marine Corps RCS DN-7321-02 applies.

b. MWR Records. The special services officer may request the plant account office to account for property procured with nonappropriated funds which meets the plant account criteria.

2. Minor Property. The activity PCO shall manage and control the acquisition of minor property (cost $5,000 or less), to include PSE.

a. Records. The property record will include the data elements shown in appendix L for minor property.

b. ADPE. The property record for a ADPE (hardware and software), whether plant or minor property, shall include the DPIC shown in appendix M.

8003. IDENTIFICATION. Garrison property is identified for management and accounting purposes through a system of unique identification (ID) and registration numbers.

1. Authority. The CMC (LFS) controls the assignment of plant account (PA) ID numbers for classes 3 and 4 plant property, minor property, and registration numbers for GME. Instructions on ID and registration numbers applicable to plant property are in the NavCompt Manual, chapter 3, paragraph 036204. The activity plant account office or the PCO shall maintain a log and control the assignment of all plant or minor property ID numbers issued to each item.

2. Criteria. Property with a unit cost of $5,000 or greater is accounted for as plant property. Property with a unit cost less than $5,000 is accounted for as minor property. Property classified as GME is accounted for through the assigned registration number as plant property.

3. Labels. All Marine Corps garrison property shall use barcoded ID labels to accommodate use of logistics applications for automated marking and reading symbols (LOGMARS) scanning equipment for physical inventory purposes. Marking or remarking on-hand property with barcoded labels should be done incrementally during the course of the quarterly reconciliation and/or the annual physical inventory, dependent on available resource. Military standards 129 and 1189 apply.

a. Label Equipment. Use available barcode printing equipment to produce all future labels. If local funds are available, labels may be commercially printed.

b. Material for Labels. A label composed of polyvinyl stock with a strong adhesive for a variety of surfaces and environments, and a protective laminate, shall be applicable for most property. The adhesive backing on the label reaches maximum adhesion 72 hours after application. A metal label is recommended for food service equipment, vehicles, heavy duty equipment, and any equipment subject to wide variations of temperature, harsh treatment, or constant handling. Label quality is the most critical factor to ensure the success of planned scanning for inventory. MCO P7300.8 provides further guidance.

c. Assignment of Numbers. The numbers used for the assignment are determined as follows.

(1) Plant Property

(a) New Property. Assign new plant property the next available PA ID number.

(b) Existing Property. If the current PA ID number on existing plant property were assigned to the present command, relabel the property with the same number. If the current PA ID on property does not have a valid ID number, relabel the property with the next assigned number.

(c) Transferred Property. If the plant property was transferred from another command, relabel the property with the number originally assigned. The possessor code on the DoD property record must reflect the unique identification code (UIC) of the command in possession of the property.

(d) Invalid ID. If the current PA ID on equipment is not a valid ID number assigned to a command, relabel with the next assigned number.

(2) Minor Property. Expendable items, such as sheets, pillow cases, mattress covers, and bedspreads, need not be marked.

d. Marking on Labels. Alternate the information line sequence, if necessary, to accommodate existing in-house barcode label printing equipment. Labels should contain the following information:

(1) Plant Property

(a) First Line. The first line should contain the abbreviation: "USMC."

(b) Second Line. The second line should contain a 12-digit barcoded identification number consisting of an "M" (1-digit); a unit identification code of the activity where the equipment is placed in use for the first time (five digits) (for example M00318); and an identification suffix (six digits). Where the unit identification code of the activity does not comprise 5 digits, zeros shall be inserted preceding the significant numbers. A sample PA number is "M00318525125."

(c) Third Line. The third line should contain the words: "Plant Property."

(2) Minor Property. NavCompt Manual, paragraph 036702, directs marking minor property.

(a) First Line. The first line should containthe abbreviation: "USMC."

(b) Second Line. The second line should contain a 12-digit barcoded ID number consisting of two alpha characters to designate the activity and a 10-digit serial number. A sample minor property number is "HQ0000005691."

(c) Third Line. The third line should contain the words: "Minor Property."

(d) ID. Minor property is accounted for with a unique block of ID numbers for each activity, as shown in appendix I. Other commands should contact CMC (LFS) for assignment of ID numbers.

(e) ADPE. Activities shall physically tag all accessory and auxiliary ADPE with a unique ID number.

(3) GME. Tag centrally-managed GME with the barcoded registration number on the label. Do not issue a separate PA ID number. The format for the label is:

(a) First Line. The first line should contain the abbreviation: "USMC."

(b) Second Line. The second line should contain a 12-digit barcoded identification number consisting of "USMCGM" (6 digits) and a GME registration number for each vehicle. A sample GME number is "USMCGM274123."

(c) Third Line. The third line should contain the words: "Garrison Mobile Equipment" or "GME."

(4) MWR Property. Property owned by the recreation fund that is procured with nonappropriated funds shall continue to be identified and accounted for as indicated in MCO P1700.27. MWR property procured with appropriated funds must be accounted for as plant or minor property. The MWR RO may be delegated to serve in a dual role as the RO for garrison property procured with appropriated funds and for the other NAF MWR property used in recreation areas.

e. Placement of Labels. Place barcoded labels on property in an accessible location that does not distract from the item's appearance, interfere with performance, or invite tampering. Avoid placing labels inside, underneath, or on hidden sides or backs of items.

(1) Position. Once the correct side of an item has been identified, place the label so it can be easily read. Use the following placement order of preference: upper right corner, upper left corner, upper center, lower right corner, lower left corner, and lower center.

(2) Fit. Although not a preferred method, the label may be cut to fit small or odd-shaped items. When cutting tags to fit an item, leave a 1/4-in section on each end of the barcode to permit automated equipment to accurately read the tag. MILSTD 1189 provides guidance to ensure the accurate scanning of the labels.

(3) Axis. Place the label with its axis perpendicular to any curved surfaces. This helps to ensure that automated readings can be taken quickly and accurately.

(4) Smooth Surface. To ensure a label can be read with a light-sensitive wand scanner, place tags on a smooth surface; however, the primary importance is placing the label in an easily viewed position to facilitate visually during an inventory.

8004. PHYSICAL INVENTORY. Activities must reconcile garrison property records with assets semiannually and conduct a physical inventory of all property annually.

1. References. While the NavCompt Manual, volume 3, requires an inventory of all garrison property every 3 years, MCO P4400.150 and UM-4400-15, however, require an annual inventory of Marine Corps property. An additional or separate physical inventory above the annual inventory is not required to meet the NavCompt triennial inventory requirement. The NavCompt Manual, volume 3, chapter 6, provides instructions and procedures to conduct the annual Marine Corps inventory.

2. Responsibility. A PCO and the plant account office shall designate an inventory team, independent of the RO, to conduct the annual inventory of garrison plant and minor property. For plant account property, reconcile the records of the activity and the fiscal office within 3 months after the inventory completion. When the physical inventory results cannot be reconciled with the accountable records, the PCO or plant account office shall perform causative research and conduct investigations, as the circumstances warrant. The PCO shall take appropriate action to reconcile records as delineated in MCO P4400.150.

3. Plant Property. Conduct the annual inventory of classes 3 and 4 plant property during 2 January to 28 February. Reconcile the physical inventory results with the accountable records. Perform causative research and conduct investigations, as the circumstances warrant.

a. Class 4 Records. After the physical inventory and records reconciliation, the activity's fiscal office shall reconcile class 4 records with DIPEC and report the completion date and results to the Naval Industrial Resource Support Activity (NAVIRSA), Philadelphia, Pennsylvania, not later than 6 months after the inventory completion.

4. PSE Inventory. Conduct the annual inventory of PSE during 1 July to 15 August to facilitate submission of the PSE Annual Inventory Report (RCS DN-7110-03) to CMC (LFS). Submit the report shown in appendix L to CMC (LFS) annually on 15 September. During the annual inventory, record the condition code (defined in appendix G), on-hand quantity, and deficiencies. Use the IRBAR to generate the requirements for the PSE Annual Inventory Report shown in appendix L. The annual inventory report used for the PSE budget is discussed in chapter 6 of this Manual.

8005. TRANSFER

1. Plant Property. Report serviceable class 3 property to the CMC (LFS) before transfer. In addition to the instructions and procedures contained in the NavCompt Manual, paragraph 036305, the report should include the name of the receiving activity and a point of contact, along with a copy of the DD 1342.

2. Excess Property. Undertake transfer of excess property from one installation to another only if economically feasible. Factors to consider are accessorial and administrative costs, repair costs, suitability of property in relationship to the cost of new procurement and available funds, and time factors. Such transfers are not reimbursable, but are subject to accessorial cost charges incident to the transfer, as prescribed in paragraph 10009 of MCO P7300.8D.

3. Inter-Inventory Transfer. An installation shall transfer excess property within and among Marine Corps activities to the extent possible. Do not transfer excess from one inventory to another or from one installation to another (e.g., from BEQ/BOQ to family housing) unless the items involved are in long supply to the requirements of the transferring inventory and/or installation, and are within the authorized allowances of the receiving inventory or installation.

4. Overseas Transfer. When it is advantageous to transfer excess property from CONUS locations to overseas locations, consolidate the items designated for specific locations at a central point for processing, packing, and shipping to the extent feasible.

8006. LOAN. Activity commanders may authorize the loan of garrison property, if available, to its users for special short-term requirements. Use a "property pass" system to track the garrison property while on loan. Include the user name, location during period of loan, date loaned, expected loan period, and date of return from loan. The user takes responsibility for the use, care, and maintenance of the garrison property during the period of loan. MCO P4400.150 contains policy for temporary loans of organic property.

8007. DEPLOYMENT. Garrison property issued to FMF units while in garrison is base or station property and shall not be taken into the field unless the CMC previously approved.

1. Authority. Authority is delegated to the activity commander to approve requests to remove, transport, and use (away from the confines of the base) garrison property used in the field to support local training exercises. Equipment loans deploying on other than local training exercises or for a period exceeding 5 months are not authorized. The FMF unit shall be responsible for all maintenance required during the training period.

2. Long-Term Deployment. For equipment loans exceeding 5 months, the FMF unit shall request modification for their table of equipment (T/E) as delineated in MCO 4400.172. If an FMF unit has a mission related requirements for a nonsystem item, the unit shall submit the requirements as delineated in MCO 3900.4.

3. Accountability. Use the accountability provisions of MCO P4400.150 to ensure adequate equipment maintenance and property control during periods of deployment.

8008. MAINTENANCE AND REPAIR OF PROPERTY. Limit the maintenance and repair of garrison property to actions necessary to keep property in such condition that it may be used for its intended purpose and to protect the Government's investment.

1. Definitions

a. Maintenance. Maintenance is the scheduled cleaning, servicing, and adjustment necessary to keep property in a serviceable or satisfactory operating condition so the item may be used effectively for its designated purpose.

b. Repair. Repair is the restoration or replacement of parts or components necessitated by wear and tear, damage, or parts failure, necessary to maintain property in efficient operating condition.

c. Rehabilitation. Rehabilitation is the restoration, reconditioning, renovation, repair of serviceable but repairable, or operable property to a near-new condition.

2. Preventive Maintenance. Take appropriate steps to ensure adequate day-to-day care and preventative maintenance of garrison property. Only those personnel who have had adequate training for the task to be performed should make mechanical repairs.

3. Government Facilities. Make maximum use of cross-servicing from all Government-owned, -operated, or -contracted facilities for maintenance, when such facilities are available. Information about mandatory sources for GSA services and term contracts for maintenance, repair, and rehabilitation are in chapter 5 of MCO P4200.15G and paragraph 7004.1d of this Manual.

4. Commercial Service. Local commercial procurement of service is authorized within available funds, provided that either Government facilities are not available or the GSA or other existing Government contracts do not provide sufficient capacity. When an activity determines that services available from an existing term contract price schedule will not serve the required needs, a request to waive the requirements shall specify the quantities involved, describe the difference between the services required and those listed in the price schedule, and state why the services will not meet the requirements.

5. Selective Interchange of Parts. Disassembly of commercial-type garrison property for serviceable parts is authorized when:

a. The item has an original acquisition cost of $5,000 or

b. In the opinion of the activity commander, the item is no longer usable in its present condition and cannot be economically repaired and used for the purpose for which originally intended, and cannot be expected to realize a fair market value if used for trade-in purposes; or

c. When specifically authorized by the CMC (LFS).

6. Warranties. GSA FSS and Marine Corps contracts contain clauses on contractor performance and warranties in supply and service acquisitions. The contracting officer must comply with FAR/DFARS/NAPS part 46.7 when a Marine Corps contract is used to acquire garrison property from commercial sources. The warranty should be cost-effective and in the best interest of the Government. Equipment repair and parts included under a commercial warranty are the responsibility of the supplier or manufacturer unless the warranty is not cost-effective for the Government to enforce.

a. Inspection. Inspect new property at the time of receipt. Expeditiously report any and all discrepancies found to the applicable procuring source. Defects not reported immediately may jeopardize the Government's legal rights. See FAR/DFARS/NAPS part 46.

b. Quality Defects. Report complaints involving quality of merchandise and latent defects discovered subsequent to receipt to the procuring office. For property obtained under GSA FSS with significant or repeated complaints, notify CMC (LFS) with copies of the complaints, for liaison with GSA to obtain corrective action from the manufacturer(s).

7. Reporting. The activity exciting the contract shall report all locally executed contracts for maintenance, other than cleaning and minor adjustments, to the appropriate GSA regional office via CMC (LFS).

8009. REPLACEMENT. Request a garrison property item, approved for replacement, in the programming and budget process as directed in chapter 6 of this Manual.

1. Authorization. The activity commancer must approve a written justification supporting any replacement. Retain this justification as part of the procurement documentation file.

2. Definitions

a. Life Expectancy. Life expectancy is the estimated number of years property is expected to exist in a serviceable condition. The life expectancies of selected items are shown in appendix J. For items not listed, use the life expectancy for a similar or related category of equipment. Guidelines to determine the life expectancy of classes 3 and 4 plant property are in the NavCompt Manual, volume 3, chapter 6. Additional service life data for IPE is in DLAM 4215.1.

b. Replacement Year. The replacement year is usually the last year of an item's life expectancy. However, when the replacement year is assigned also consider other factors, such as previous use history with the same make and model equipment, IRS depreciation schedules, and manufacturer's expected life. Revise the replacement year, if at any time during the service life testing, inspection, or other local circumstances warrant.

3. Replacement Criteria. Property may be replaced under the following conditions:

a. History of Breakdowns. Property may be replaced when there is a continuing history of breakdowns with corresponding loss of productivity through downtime.

b. Cumulative Repair Costs. Property may be replaced when the cumulative repair costs appear to be excessive, based upon the personal knowledge of the supervisor and indicated by repair records. However, the fact that property has accrued repair costs equal to the acquisition cost does not necessarily indicate the current condition of the property. For example, a substantial repair expenditure included in the cumulative cost may actually have resulted in restoring the machine to as good as new condition. While cumulative repair costs suggest an area for investigation, this alone is not the principal factor in making a repair/replacement decision.

c. Repair Parts. Property may be replaced when repair parts are not available, causing property to be out of service for an excessive amount of time.

d. Essential Features. Property may be replaced when it lacks essential features required to perform a particular task that is continuing in nature and other suitable property is not readily available. However, this condition shall not be used to support the replacement of typewriters.

e. Economical Repair. Property may be replaced when properly determined beyond economical repair. Economical repair is different for various types of property.

f. Replacement Program. Property may be replaced to comply with replacement programs designed to phase out items that have reached or have exceeded their life expectancies.

4. Replacement of PSE

a. Estimated Cost. Do not replace furniture unless the estimated cost of repair or rehabilitation (based on GSA term contracts), including any transportation expense, exceeds 75 percent of the cost of a new item of the same type and class (based on prices in the GSA supply catalog, applicable FSS's, or the lowest available market price). The IRBAR (see chapter 2) will identify PSE scheduled for replacement during the 7- to 10-year cycle.

b. Unusual Conditions. An exception is authorized when a repair costing 75 percent or less of the cost of a new item would not extend the useful life.

5. Replacement of Office Machines. Acquisition costs of comparable machines may be obtained from applicable FSS's to consider prices obtainable when the quantities involved exceed the maximum order limitation. In such instances, price information may be obtained from the contracting office indicated in the schedule. Include transportation expense in the costs obtained.

a. Electrically Operated Office Machines. Electrically operated office machines, such as typewriters, adding machines, and desk calculators (excluding the electronic type) under 12 years old, or manually operated office machines under 15 years old shall not be replaced unless they meet one of the following criteria:

(1) Under 8 Years Old. The estimated one-time repair or overhaul cost of a machine under 8 years old must exceed 50 percent of the replacement cost for a comparable new model, without regard to trade-in or sale value.

(2) Over 8 Years Old. The estimated one-time repair or overhaul cost of a machine 8 years old or over must exceed 25 percent of the replacement cost for a comparable new model, without regard to trade-in or sale value.

b. Electronic Office Machines. Electronic office machines, such as calculators, accounting machines, and cash registers, shall be replaced after expiration of the warranty period if repair cost exceed 80 percent of the replacement cost of a comparable new model.

8010. DISPOSAL

1. Excess Property

a. Definition. Excess property is any personnel property under the control of the activity commander or his designee determined not to be required to discharge the command responsibilities.

b. Redistribution. Use existing stocks of Government-owned usable garrison property to the fullest extent practicable for authorized requirements. To this end, transfer property excess to requirements of an installation within and among Marine Corps activities, and between the family housing inventories and the BEQ/BOQ inventories. See paragraph 8005 of this Manual for transfer guidance. Transfers of furniture are not reimbursable, but are subject to accessorial and/or administrative cost charges incident to transfer, as prescribed in paragraph 10009 of MCO P11000.12C.

c. Other DoD Components. The CMC (LFS) will direct the redistribution of excess garrison property available at Marine Corps activities to other DoD components. The redistribution will be to meet requirements with suitable Government-owned items in lieu of new procurement, whenever this is economically advantageous.

2. Serviceable Property

a. Serviceable Excess or Idle Class 3 Property. Serviceable class 3 property must be reported to the CMC (LFS) before transfer to disposal. Whenever possible, this equipment will be redistributed to satisfy other Marine Corps requirements. If excess or idle equipment is not required, disposition instructions will be provided. Instructions and reporting procedures for the transfer of class 3 plant property are in the NavCompt Manual, paragraph 036305. A copy of the DD 1342 indicating the current condition code and reason for turn-in should be submitted with the request for disposition instructions.

b. Class 4 (IPE) Property. The DIPEC is responsible to control and dispose of all DoD IPE. The NavCompt Manual, paragraph 0364087, and MCO 4500.11 contain guidance for the disposal of unserviceable and serviceable excess or idle class 4 IPE. Submit requests to dispose of class 4 IPE to DIPEC via CMC (LFS).

c. Minor Property. Transfer serviceable property excess to requirements of an installation within and among Marine Corps activities. The CMC (LFS) will direct the redistribution of excess garrison property available at a Marine Corps activity. The redistribution will meet requirements with suitable Government-owned items in lieu of new procurement, whenever this is economically advantageous. Minor property not redistributed to another activity shall comply with the instructions in MCO 4500.11 and shall be turned over to the nearest DRMO for disposal.

3. Unserviceable Property

a. Class 3 Property. When class 3 property becomes obsolete, unfit for performance, or unserviceable through no specific cause or as a consequence of normal use it shall be turned over to the DRMO.

b. Minor Property. Disposition of minor property shall comply with the instructions contained in MCO 4500.11.

4. Repair of Excess Property. Do not expend funds to clean, repair, maintain, or replace excess property. Remove excess furnishings requiring repair from quarters or warehouse stocks for disposal. Take prompt action to dispose of excess property beyond the economical repair criteria.

8011. PROPERTY REPORTS

1. Quarterly Reports. Activities shall submit a quarterly CSE PMC report (RCS DN-7321-04) before the 10th day of October, January, April, and July of each year to indicate the status of authorized procurement in the format entitled "CSE Status Report," shown in appendix L, to the CMC (LFS). Submit a separate report for each appropriation line, such as Report Control Number (RCN) 06001 or 06342. Retain a copy of the quarterly status report for 1 year after submission.

2. Semiannual Plant Property Reports

a. Purpose. HQMC uses the semiannual plant property to substantiate the cost data reflected on the Reconciliation of Plant Account (NavCompt Form 167), determine projected equipment replacement requirements for budget purposes, and ensure plant property accountability of the entire Marine Corps equipment inventory.

b. Report Submission. The NavCompt Manual, volume 3, chapter 6, defines the criteria used to determine plant property classes. All Marine Corps-owned property defined as class 3 and 4 will be included in the inventory report, except those items specifically exempted. The class 3 and 4 plant property report shall be submitted in separate property class and in standard commodity code (SCC) or plant equipment code (PEC) sequence. A class 1 and 2 property listing is no longer submitted to HQMC.

c. Format. Prepare and submit the semiannual plant property report (RCS-DN-7321-01) using the general guidance and format shown in appendix L.

d. Responsibility. The activities in appendix M shall submit the plant property report for all accountable plant property semiannually before 15 April and 15 October to:

Commandant of the Marine Corps (FDL)
Headquarters, U.S. Marine Corps
Washington, DC 20380-0001

e. Report Retention. Submitting activities shall retain a copy of the semiannual plant property report for a period of 2 years after submission.

3. NavCompt Form 167. The fiscal office for each plant account activity (PAA) shall prepare a quarterly summary of the plant property monetary value on the Reconciliation of Plant Account (NavCompt Form 167). Marine Corps activities shall submit the report (RCS-DN-7321-02) for all property regardless of funding source on a single report to CMC (FDL). The NavCompt Manual, paragraph 036515, provides instructions for submitting this report, due the 18th day following the end of each quarter.

APPENDIX A

REFERENCES

(a) DLAM 4215.1, Management of Defense-Owned Industrial Plant Equipment

(b) DoD 4165.63M, DoD Housing Management (P&L)

(c) DoD Manual 7950.1-M, Defense Automation Resources Management Manual

(d) Federal Acquisition Regulations (FAR)

(e) Federal Property Management Regulations (FPMR)

(f) Furniture Catalog, GSA, FSS

(g) GSA Supply Catalog

(h) Joint Federal Travel Regulations (JFTR)

(i) MCO P1700.27, Marine Corps Morale, Welfare and Recreation Manual

(j) MCO 1710.30, Child Care Center Policy and Operational Guidelines

(k) MCO 3900.4, Marine Corps Program Initiation and Operational Requirement Documents

(l) MCO P4064.3, Marine Corps Laundry Manual

(m) MCO P4200.15, Marine Corps Purchasing Procedures Manual

(n) MCO 4225.2 Musical Instruments and Accessories

(o) MCO P4400.150, Consumer Level Supply Policy Manual

(p) MCO 4400.172, Table of Equipment (T/E) Allowance Change Procedures

(q) MCO P4450.7, Marine Corps Warehousing Manual

(r) MCO 4450.10, Storage and Warehousing Operations and Equipment Modernization Planning and Programming

(s) MCO 4500.11, Instructions for Disposition/Utilization of Excess Personal Property

(t) MCO P4733.1, Marine Corps Test, Measurement and Diagnostic Equipment (TMDE) Calibration and Maintenance Program (CAMP)

(u) MCO 4860.3, Operation of Commercial- and Industrial-Type Activities

(v) MCO 5030.3, Unofficial Use of the Seal, Emblem, Names or Initials of the Marine Corps

(w) MCO 5210.11, Record Management Program for the Marine Corps

(x) MCO 5210.13 (Microform Management), Marine Corps Microform Management Program

(y) MCO P5230.10, Automated Data Processing for the FMF Management Plan

(z) MCO P5230.15, Data Base Administration

(aa) MCO P5290.1, USMC Training and Audiovisual Support Manual

(bb) MCO P5600.31, Marine Corps Publication and Printing Regulations

(cc) MCO 7000.12, Economic Analysis

(dd) MCO P7100.8, Field Budget Guidance Manual

(ee) MCO P7300.8, Financial Accounting Manual

(ff) MCO P10110.14, Food Service and Subsistence Management Manual

(gg) MCO P10110.34, Food Service and Subsistence Program

(hh) MCO 10510.18, Policy and Responsibility for Test, Measurement and Diagnostic Equipment (TMDE)

(ii) MCO P11000.5, Real Property Facilities Manual, Vol. IV

(jj) MCO P11000.9, Real Property Facilities Manual, Vol. VI

(kk) MCO P11000.12, Real Property Facilities Manual, Vol. II

(ll) MCO P11000.22, Marine Corps Housing Management Manual

(mm) MCO P11240.106, Garrison Mobile Equipment

(nn) MCO 11310.10, Mobile Electric Power Generators

(oo) Military Standard (MILSTD) 1189A

(pp) Military Standard (MILSTD) 129

(qq) MIL-C-4150

(rr) Navy Comptroller (NavCompt) Manual

(ss) NAVFACINST 11010.74, Collateral Equipment Required to Initially Outfit Military Construction, Navy and Military Construction Naval Reserve Projects

(tt) NAVSUP PUB 529, Warehouse Modernization and Layout Planning Guide

(uu) OPNAV 5530.15, Military Police Physical Security

(vv) SECNAVINST 5030.4, Official Establishment of Department of Navy Seal (ww) UM-4400-15, Organic Property Control Procedures Users Manual

(xx) UM-4400-124, FMF SASSY Using Unit Procedures Users Manual

APPENDIX B

ACRONYMS

AAN	Accountable Activity Number
ACR	Allowance Change Requests
ADP	Automated Data Processing
ADPE	Automated Data Processing Equipment
APA	Appropriation Purchase Account
APF	Appropriated Fund
BEQ	Bachelor Enlisted Quarters
BOD	Beneficial Occupancy Date
BOQ	Bachelor Officers Quarters
BPCO	Base Property Control Office
BY	Budget Year
CDC	Child Development Center
CE	Collateral Equipment
CG MCCDC	Commanding General, Marine Corps Combat Development Command, Quantico
CMC	Commandant of the Marine Corps
CNA	Certificate of Nonavailability
CONUS	Continental United States
CSE	Command Support Equipment
DIPEC	Defense Industrial Plant Equipment Center
DLA	Defense Logistics Agency
DMA	Depot Maintenance Activities
DoD	Department of Defense
DON	Department of the Navy
DPIC	Data Processing Installation Code

DRIS	Defense Regional Interservice Support
DRMO	Defense Reutilization and Marketing Office
DRMS	Defense Reutilization and Marketing Service
DSS-W	Defense Supply Service-Washington
E	Enlisted
EA	Economic Analysis
EFD	Engineering Field Division
EUCE	End-User Computer Equipment
FAR	Federal Acquisition Regulations
FMF	Fleet Marine Force
FPI	Federal Prison Industries
FPMR	Federal Property Management Regulations
FPSE	Food Preparation and Serving Equipment
FSC	Federal Supply Class
FSS	Federal Supply Schedules
FY	Fiscal Year
GME	Garrison Mobile Equipment
GRIP	General Reserve Interrogation Program
GS	General Schedule
GSA	General Services Administration
HD	Marine Corps History and Museums, Headquarters Marine Corps
HQMC	Headquarters Marine Corps
ID	Identification
IDS	Intrusion Detection System
IPE	Industrial Plant Equipment

IRBAR	Inventory, Requirements, Budget, and Replacement Plan
JFIP	Japanese Facility Improvement Program
JFTR	Joint Federal Travel Regulations
JUMPS	Joint Uniformed Military Pay System
LFF	Facilities Branch, Installations and Logistics Department, Headquarters Marine Corps
LFL	Land Use and Military Construction Branch, Installations and Logistics Department, Headquarters Marine Corps
LFS	Services Branch, Installations and Logistics Department, Headquarters Marine Corps
LUAF	Loaded Unit Allowance File
MAL	Mechanized Allowance List
MCCTA (CTAR)	Marine Corps Computer and Telecommunications Activity Computer Division, Information Resources Management Section
MCLB	Marine Corps Logistics Base
MCNR	Military Construction Naval Reserve
MCO	Marine Corps Order
MCON CE	Collateral Equipment in Military Construction
MFC	Manufacturer Code
MFIP	Messhall Facility Improvement Program
MFR	Manufacturer
MHE	Materials Equipment Handling
MILCON	Military Construction
MMS	Manpower Management System
MOL	Maximum Order Limitation
MP	Minor Property
MSA	Minimum Standards of Adequacy
MRP	Maintenance of Real Property
MWR	Morale, Welfare, and Recreation

NAF	Nonappropriated Fund
NAVFACENGCOM	Commander, Naval Facilities Engineering Command
NAVIRSA	Naval Industrial Resources Support Activity
NCO	Noncommissioned Officer
NCR	National Capitol Region
NSN	National Stock Number
O&MMC	Operation and Maintenance, Marine Corps
O&MMCR	Operation and Maintenance, Marine Corps Reserve
OCR	Optical Character Reader
OFRM	Officer's Field Ration Messhall
OISE	Office Information Systems Equipment
OPBUD	Operating Budget
PA	Plant Account
PAA	Plant Account Activity
PCS	Permanent Change of Station
PCO	Property Control Officer
PD	Procurement Documentation
PEC	Plant Equipment Code
PED	Project Engineering Documentation
PHSE	Physical Security Equipment
PMC	Procurement, Marine Corps
POM	Program Objective Memorandum
POS	Security Branch Department, Headquarters Marine Corps
PPBS	Planning, Programming, and Budgeting System
PSE	Personnel Support Equipment
RCN	Report Control Number

RO	Responsible Officer
RUAF	Reporting Unit Allowance File
SCC	Standard Commodity Code
SE	Supporting Establishment
SES	Senior Executive Service
SNCO	Staff Non-Commissioned Officer
T/E	Table of Equipment
TAM	Table of Authorized Material
TAMCN	Table of Authorized Material Control Number
TAVIS	Training and Audiovisual Information Support
TAVSC	Training and Audiovisual Information Support Center
UIC	Unit Identification Code
UL	Underwriters Laboratory
UMC	Unspecified Minor Construction
UPS	Uninterruptible Power Supply
USMCGM	United States Marine Corps Garrison Mobile
Whse Mod	Warehouse Modernization
WPE	Word Processing Equipment

APPENDIX C

PSE ITEM DESCRIPTIONS

1. Air-Conditioners. Air-conditioning equipment of any size is not considered furnishings or household equipment. Authorization and installation of air-conditioning shall comply with MCO P11000.9. Air-conditioning equipment is not funded with PSE funds, but with local maintenance or repair funds.

2. Bedding. Bedding includes the bed (bedframe, headboard, bedspring, and mattress) and linens (bedspread, mattress cover and pad, pillow and pillow cases, and sheets). All linens except bedspreads are procured with local funds.

a. Beds

(1) Metal Bunk Beds. Metal bunk beds (regular or extra-length), with sinuous-type springs and innerspring mattresses, are the standard for the recruit trainee in open squad bay areas. The beds may be used singly or in double-bunk fashion. When double bunking is selected, adapter sets should be ordered in the same color to assure a perfect color match. The military standard bunk bed is covered by Military Specification MIL-B-15228E. The bed may be provided with headboard and footboard panels, conforming to Military Specification MIL-P-28638A (YD) and with a bunk shelf conforming to MIL-B-28635A (YD) where appropriate.

(2) v. Conventional beds include a spring, mattress, frame, headboard, and footboard. Conventional beds are recommended in BEQ/BOQ transient facilities. The following allowance is authorized for conventional beds used in motel style and in converted, open squad bay units, contingent on available quarters and space:

Rank	Size
E1-E5	Single
E6-E9	Double
CW01-CW04	Double
01-05	Double
06 and above	Queen

(3) Hollywood Beds. Hollywood beds (conventional beds without footboards) may be used in lieu of conventional beds.

(4) Convertible Beds. Convertible sofas or hide-a-beds for studio rooms and one-room apartments offer the dual function of bed and sofa. Convertible beds may be authorized when the rank of the occupant justifies space for a suite or for larger quarters

b. Bedspreads. The purpose of the bedspread is to keep the blanket, bed linens, and bedding clean and dust free and to improve the overall appearance of the room. All beds shall be covered with a washable, lint-free, flame-retardant fabric bedspread when not in use.

(1) Allowance. An allowance of two bedspreads per bed is authorized. The bedspread shall not be a substitute for but shall be in addition to the minimum blanket allowance (one each). Initial outfitting for new or renovated BEQ/BOQ facilities should identify bedspread quantity and NSN for procurement through GSA.

(2) Size and Color. The bedspread shall be draped over the bed and will hang approximately 6 inches above the floor on 3 sides, with sufficient material to tuck under the pillow. Extra-length bedspreads are recommended for extra-length beds. A variety of solid color bedspreads is available in the GSA Supply Catalog (Industrial Products).

c. Bedsprings. Bedsprings must be enclosed box springs (set in ticking). Open bedsprings are not acceptable.

d. Mattresses. Mattresses shall be of the same width and length as their accompanying box springs to avoid damage to either item.

(1) Fire Retardancy. Fire retardancy for mattress pads is generally effective through 10 washings. Local laundry facilities can restore fire retardancy during the washing process to reduce acquisition costs.

(2) Maintenance. The PCO should establish a program to have the mattresses professionally cleaned once every 2 to 3 years. The replacement of the ticking and mattress contents through a commercial refurbishment process is recommended every 4 to 5 years to prolong the life expectancy of the mattress. Use funds authorized from the CMC or local funds for this purpose.

(3) Transfer. When a room or bed assignment is transferred from one person to another, the mattress should be new or just cleaned.

e. Mattress Pads. Keep mattresses covered with mattress pads and covers to avoid spoilage and damage. Mattress pads or covers (two for each bed) should be on hand at all times for use on bedding to maintain clean and sanitary conditions and to prolong the bedding life expectancy.

f. Pillows and Pillow Cases. Cover pillows with pillow cases to avoid spoilage and damage. Pillows of polyester-filled nonallergenic or flaked urethane-filled, washable, with flame-retardant properties are authorized.

(1) Inspection. Inspect all pillows and mattresses at least semiannually at a minimum to maintain cleanliness and serviceability standards.

(2) Fire Retardancy. Fire retardancy is generally effective only through 10 washings. Local laundry facilities are able to restore fire retardancy during the washing process.

g. Sheets. Cover mattresses with top and bottom sheets.

3. Fans. Fans may be authorized where air-conditioning is not available and climatic conditions make it desirable. Ceiling fans are not PSE. Requirements for ceiling fans should comply with public works or facilities office policy for built-in equipment. Fans shall be UL-approved. Criteria for fans are:

Floor Fan	-	1 per lounge 1 per 500 ft(2) barrack
Desk Fan	-	1 per 150 ft(2) barracks 1 per bedroom bachelors' quarters 1 per living room or living room combination, if not otherwise provided in bachelors' quarters

4. Fire Extinguisher and Ironing Boards. Fire extinguishers and ironing boards with covers are authorized as required for safety and convenience.

5. Floor Covering

a. Carpet. Carpet (or floor covering) becomes part of the facility. The office charged with the maintenance of real property (MRP) shall procure carpet only for maintenance, repair, or improvement to the facility. Carpet is not an item of furnishings. Procurement of carpet with PSE funds is not authorized.

(1) Justification. Carpet is authorized for use in office spaces where it can be justified over other types of floor covering on the basis of cost, safety, insulation, acoustical control, appearance, or maintenance of an environment commensurate with the purpose for which the space is allocated. If during a construction or renovation project, it is known the area will eventually require carpeting, then noncarpet floor covering should be omitted and carpet installed initially.

(2) Authorization. Wall-to-wall carpet is authorized only when the CMC (LFF) provides approval.

b. Rugs. Rugs which are not affixed to a facility are considered items of furnishings and are authorized for use in BEQ/BOQ spaces. Use short pile, closely woven rugs with attached rubber cushioning. Do not use loose pile and shag rugs.

(1) Source and Size. Each carpet contractor on the FSS publishes a brochure with prices of made-up, bound rugs in the more popular sizes. Take care to specify sizes to avoid waste and additional make-up charges. Rugs may not be custom-fitted. They must remain freestanding so they can be turned to achieve even wear.

(2) Cushions. Furnish rug cushions for all rugs more than 3 by 6 feet that have no protective backing.

(3) Safety. The rug system (rug and underlay) must pass a flooring radiant panel test (FRPT), or pass the UL Chamber Test (UL 992) with a flame propagation index of less than 4.0.

(4) Color. Use care to select the appropriate color and pile for both rugs and carpet. For the greatest wear and maintainability, choose medium shades in either a solid color or pattern.

6. Footlockers. Footlockers (plywood barracks locker trunks) or locker boxes (formerly listed in the TAM) are being phased out in favor of wardrobes. They may continue to be used in recruit quarters as substitutes for wardrobes but shall not be used or replaced in other unaccompanied housing areas. Footlockers currently available in other areas may be used until worn out.

7. Lamps. Use lamps with leather-covered, metal, wood, or combination wood/metal bases. Do not use glass or ceramic lamps. Swing-arm lamps often are poorly balanced and are not recommended. Lamps with molded or other plastic dome or globe shades are considered hazardous and shall not be procured. Table and floor lamps may be substituted for each other. New lamps should be examined for faulty wiring, switches, and construction. Lamps with faulty switches and frayed wires should be replaced immediately. All lamps must be UL-approved.

a. Table Lamps. Determine the size of table lamps by their purpose or by the furniture item on which they are placed: small lamps on night tables, study lamps on desks, medium size lamps on end tables, and extra-tall lamps on large furniture items or in rooms having high ceilings.

b. Floor Lamps. Use large floor lamps in areas requiring bright lighting, areas having high ceilings, or where large-scale furniture is used. Small floor lamps should be considered under other conditions. All floor lamps should have a firm, heavy base.

c. Lamp Shades and Globes. Use lamp shades of fiberglass or paper parchment. Use paper parchment shades when opaque shades are required to direct light, such as in television rooms. Fiberglass shades provide a more uniform distribution of light for general purpose areas. Lamp shades should conform to the size of the lamp. Lamps should have metal harps in lieu of glass globes, when practicable. Procure and stock extra glass globes and lamp shades.

d. Bulbs. Do not procure lamps having bulb wattage limitations if 100 watt bulbs cannot be used safely. Do not procure lamps requiring special bulbs unless the supply activity supporting the user can assure proper bulbs for initial use and replacement. Three-way lamp bulbs should be furnished for three-way lamps and extra bulbs should be stocked. All incandescent lamp fixtures should be able to use a GSA approved screw-in fluorescent bulb of equivalent lumens without modifications to the lamp and without extending the shade or dome of the lamp.

8. Microwave Ovens. Microwave ovens are authorized as follows:

a. Common Kitchen Areas. Microwave ovens are authorized in common kitchen areas that are equipped for food preparation with the standard kitchen appliances, stove, refrigerator, dishwasher, and garbage disposal, and with an area set aside for dining. Use appropriated maintenance/repair funds available for built-in equipment. Do not use PSE funds to procure microwave ovens.

b. BEQ/BOQ. Microwave ovens are authorized for BEQ/BOQ sleeping or living areas only when a specific area is equipped with adequate electrical, plumbing, sanitary, and safety facilities to accommodate the equipment.

(1) Transient Quarters -- Use nonappropriated billeting funds when a microwave oven is used in a common area.

(2) Permanent Party Quarters -- Microwave ovens which are personal property of the occupant in permanent party quarters may be used if the criteria in paragraph 8a above are met.

c. Administrative Offices. Microwave ovens for employees' personal use in administrative offices must be procured with personal funds. Appropriated funds may not be used for this purpose.

9. Mirrors. Standard-size mirrors are authorized for dressers or chests of drawers. Full-length mirrors are authorized for all sleeping quarters. To avoid breakage, glassless mirrors are recommended. Check GSA schedules for the availability of sizes and types. Where rate of issue is on the basis of "one per two," one mirror is permissible for single occupancy rooms, and two mirrors are permissible in three-person rooms, space permitting.

10. Modular Cabinetry or Wall Furniture. Modular cabinetry is designed to furnish maximum living and storage space within a limited amount of floor space. It offers an attractive and practical unit in sleeping areas and reduces the number of separate pieces of furniture. Modular cabinets should also be considered in small lounge applications.

11. Personal Convenience Items. Do not use PSE funds to procure personal convenience items, such as flat irons, hair dryers, bedboards, individual radios, and television sets. Procure these items with personal funds.

12. Pictures and Other Wall Decor. Initial outfitting of pictures and wall decor for common areas such as lounges and waiting areas in messhalls is authorized using MCON CE funds provided for that purpose. Subsequent replacement pictures and wall decor are procured with command funds.

a. Sources. Good, reasonably priced wall decor, including original art and reproductions of paintings and pictures in all media, is available through national and local artwork distributors. A variety of artwork and wall decoration is available in the FSS.

b. Selection. Choice of pictures and murals shall match the decor of the building and its furnishings. Materials used shall be suitable for the geographic area. Keep costs to a reasonable level, yet provide sufficient quality to ensure durability.

c. Individual Decor. Government-furnished wall decor is not provided for BEQ/BOQ living quarters or sleeping areas. Using personal funds, individuals should be allowed to furnish their own pictures, paintings, and decor in sleeping areas or offices, consistent with local regulations regarding size and placement.

13. Recreation Equipment (Morale Support-Type Equipment). Appropriated funds may be used to procure recreation-type items, such as console television sets, pool tables, and ping-pong tables used in lounges and recreation rooms in BEQ/BOQ. The expense and investment criteria apply. When appropriated funds are used for procurement, recreation equipment must be accounted for as plant or minor property. If the equipment is procured with nonappropriated funds for initial outfitting or replacement follow the instructions in MCO P1700.27.

14. Refrigerators. Refrigerators are available for convenience items such as milk, juice, fruit, bread, cheese, and ice cream. They are not intended to replace messhall, club, or other designated kitchen facilities.

a. BEQ/BOQ. One refrigerator, not to exceed 5.5 ft(3), is authorized in each occupied room or suite of rooms in BEQ/BOQ. Where more than one Marine occupies a room, the refrigerator shall be shared. In new BEQ/BOQ facilities, the refrigerator shall be included as collateral equipment; in existing facilities, the refrigerator shall be procured or replaced with PSE or command funds.

b. Administrative Offices. Refrigerators for employees' personal use in administrative offices may not be procured with appropriated funds. Employees may procure refrigerators, not to exceed 5.5 ft(3), with personal funds.

15. Room Dividers. Movable or semipermanent dividers or partitions may be considered to separate cubicles in open-style quarters where construction of permanent walls is not planned.

16. Tables. Tables must be of durable quality.

17. Trophy Cases. Trophies and historic items may be stored in built-in or stand-alone cabinets or cases. Procure solid wood and glass cabinets, with good quality lock mechanisms for security. Catalog the contents and register with the activity PCO. The activity is authorized to procure cabinets with local funds for initial outfitting and for replacement. Request disposition instructions from CMC (HD) for any historic items before disposal.

18. Upholstered Seating. Upholstered seating includes sofas, sofabeds, and chairs with a fabric covering. Do not procure upholstered seating with detachable or reversible cushions unless the cushions can be secured to the furniture. Where extra hard use of the furniture is expected, expanded vinyl is recommended. Place upholstered seating only where authorized, as described below:

a. Sofas. Sofas are authorized for use in lounges, in living areas in suites for officers, and in designated staff noncommissioned officers (SNCO) quarters, space permitting. A sofa (two- or three-seat) is authorized only in Flag/SES level offices and as an option for Col/GM-15 offices in supervisory positions. Sofas or sofa beds are not authorized in any other office. Side chairs are authorized for other office spaces as indicated appendix E.

b. Sofabeds. Sofabeds may be substituted for sofas used in living quarters in BEQ/BOQ.

19. Wardrobes. Wardrobes conforming to military specification MIL-W-28581 (YD) are standard and should be built into new construction as part of the construction contract. When practical and where otherwise needed, these wardrobes should be furnished as quarters are upgraded. Provide a small three-drawer chest conforming to MIL-C-28580 (YD) for each wardrobe.

a. Metal Wardrobes. Metal wardrobes are preferred for open (squad-bay) type living quarters. Consider metal gauge thickness and durability of construction for the security of the individual's personal property when selecting this type wardrobe.

b. Other Lockers. Gymnasium-type lockers, metal storage cabinets, and other steel lockers shall no longer be procured for use as wardrobes. Existing items may be used, where required, to temporarily form cubicles in open-type quarters. Such lockers should, however, be in good condition and painted to enhance the surrounding area.

20. Washers and Dryers. Provide washers and dryers for the exclusive use of occupants of BEQ/BOQ at no cost to the occupant.

a. Selection Alternative. Washers and dryers may be Government-owned or -leased. Alternatives available include:

(1) Government-owned; maintenance by public works.

(2) Government-owned; maintenance by civilian contractor.

(3) Concessionaire-owned or -leased; maintenance by civilian contractor.

b. Contract Services. Provision of washer-dryer service under contract arrangements may be of greatest benefit and least cost to the Government. Instances may occur where contractual services are not available or when these services are not as economical as providing Government-owned equipment. In these and other unusual circumstances, Government ownership and/or operation may be authorized.

c. Economic Analysis. Before acquisition of washers and dryers by purchase or lease, the contracting officer shall complete an economic analysis and the written determination required in the FAR and MCO P4200.15, as applicable. A copy of this determination shall be filed with the procurement action. The economic analysis shall not be limited to a few equipment items but shall compare the relative advantages of operation of a complete facility with concessionaire-owned or -leased equipment to Government-owned equipment.

d. Authorization. Government-owned washers and dryers shall not be provided unless the activity commander determines it is in the best interests of the Government in each specific instance. This authority shall not be delegated below the major command level, usually the property control officer.

e. Exception. Marine Corps exchange-operated laundromat-type facilities not installed in bachelor quarters, but provided for the general use of all military personnel and their dependents, are excluded from the guidance of this Manual.

f. Instructions. Post instructions detailing procedures for laundering and equipment use conspicuously, detailing procedures above washers and dryers in enlarged lettering.

g. Replacement. Government-owned washers and dryers presently installed may continue to be used until they are no longer economically reparable. The activity commander must approve the procurement of Government-owned equipment for either new installation or replacement purposes.

21. Wastebaskets. Wastebaskets to hold paper, trash, or other debris pending disposal are authorized for use in BEQ/BOQ, administrative offices and messhalls.

22. Window Coverings

a. Blinds. Blinds, both horizontal and vertical, as part of a facility, are classified as built-in equipment. PSE funds shall not be used to procure blinds, but shall be procured with MRP funds.

b. Curtains and Drapes. Curtains and drapes may be used when justified over other types of window coverings on the basis of cost, insulation, acoustical control, or to maintain an environment commensurate with the purpose for which the space is allocated.

(1) Public Spaces and BEQ/BOQ. Curtains and drapes sufficient for reasonable coverage are authorized for public spaces, such as lounges. Fixed panel curtains or drapes are authorized for average size bedroom and living room windows with venetian blinds for BOQ's and for windows with venetian blinds in sleeping spaces of BEQ's.

(2) Administrative Offices. Venetian blinds or mini-blinds are the customary window covering for windows in administrative offices. Curtains and drapes shall not be procured for this purpose. Use of curtains and drapes on the same window with blinds in administrative offices is prohibited.

(3) Initial Outfitting. Curtains and drapes shall be provided as initial outfitting in a new or renovated BEQ/BOQ facility. Include curtain rods and installation in the cost. Procure curtains and drapes with PSE funds.

(4) Traverse Drapes. Traverse drapes with lightproof linings may be provided in bedrooms of installations in those geographical areas which have periods of prolonged daylight and high temperatures. For other conditions, the CMC (LFS) may authorize traverse drapes.

(5) Flame Retardancy. Purchase curtains and drapes of noncombustible or flame-retardant fabric. Material consisting of man-made fibers which are not flammable, but which emit vaporous gases when exposed to fumes, shall not be used.

(6) Cleaning. Professionally dry-clean curtains and drapes once a year using PSE funds. Replacement curtains and drapes are procured with PSE funds.

APPENDIX D
TABLE OF ALLOWANCES--BEQ/BOQ

1. Allowances for BEQ: Sleeping Spaces

Item	Basis of Issue
* Bed, conventional	1 per individual
* Bedspread	2 per bed
*Blanket	1 per bed (up to 2 additional blankets authorized in cold climates)
Bookcase	1 per room (if not built-in)
* Chair, desk	1 per desk
Chair, easy	1 per individual
* Cover, mattress	2 per mattress
Desk	1 per individual
* Desk wall unit (secretary) or Chest, 4 drawers	1 per individual
Lamp, floor	1 per room
* Lamp, table	1 per night table
Mirror	1 per chest of drawers
* Mirror (full length)	1 per room or suite
* Pad, mattress	1 per bed
* Pillow, bed	1 per bed
* Pillowcase	2 per pillow
* Refrigerator	1 per room or suite
* Rug, floor	Reasonable coverage
* Rug pad	1 per rug (over 3 by 6 ft)
* Sheet, bed	4 per bed or as appropriate in recruit, reception, and induction activities
* Table, night	1 per bed
Table, end	1 per two easy chairs
Table, coffee	1 per room, space permitting
* Wardrobe	1 per individual, if built-in is not provided
* Wastebasket	1 per room
* Wastebasket	1 per bath

* Indicates minimum allowance to be provided.

2. Allowances for BEQ: Lounges. A lounge is a community living room for use by all occupants of a facility. The following allowances apply to lounges of up to 400 ft(2) in size.(1)

Item	Basis of Issue
Bookcase	1 per room
Cabinet, storage	1 per room
* Chair, easy	4 per room
Chair, folding	4 per room
Chair, lounge	3 per room
Chair, straight	6 per room
Clock, wall	1 per room (as required)
Costume or coat rack	2 per room
* Sofa	2 per room
Desk	1 per room when not sleeping space
Lamp, desk	1 per desk
* Lamp, table	1 per occasional table
Lamp, floor	2 per room
Mirror, framed	1 per room
Pictures, framed	4 per room
Ping-Pong Table	1 per designated(1) game room
Pool Table	1 per designated(1) game room
* Rug, floor	Reasonable coverage
* Rug, pad	1 per rug (over 3 by 6 ft)
* Table, coffee	2 per room
* Table, general purpose	1 per room
* Table, occasional	6 per room
* Television with VCR	2 per designated(1) TV room
* Wastebasket	1 per room

3. Allowances for BOQ, Transient Officer Housing: Bedroom Suites

Item	Basis of Issue
* Bed, conventional	1 per individual
* Blanket, bed	1 per bed. Two additional may be authorized in cold climates.
Chair, easy	1 per room (when private living room not available)
* Chair, desk	1 desk
* Cover, mattress	2 per mattress
* Desk	1 per individual (when wall unit not available)
* Dresser or Chest of Drawers	1 per individual
Lamp, floor	1 per room
* Lamp, table	1 per night table and occasional table
Lamp, desk	1 per desk
* Mattress pad	1 per bed
Mirror, framed	1 per dresser or chest of drawers
* Mirror, full length	1 per room or suite
* Picture, framed	2 per room

(1)For larger lounges, the CMC (LFS) will determine the type and quantity of PSE.

Item	Basis of Issue
* Pillow, bed	1 per bed
* Pillowcase	2 per pillow
* Refrigerator	1 per room or suite
* Rug, floor	1 reasonable coverage
* Rug pad	1 per rug (over 3 by 6 ft)
* Sheet, bed	4 per bed or as appropriate in recruit reception and induction activity
Rack, luggage	1 per bed in transient quarters
* Sofa	1 per room (when not in bedroom)
* Table, night	1 per bed
Table, occasional	1 per room
* Wardrobe	1 per individual (when not built-in) (Additional storage may be authorized to meet special requirements.)
* Wastebasket	1 per room, including bathroom
* Wastebasket	1 per bath

4. Allowances for BOQ, Transient Office Housing: Living Room Suites. A "living room suite" is a suite of bedroom and living room without kitchen facilities, whether for private or joint use.

Item	Basis of Issue
Bookcase	1 per room (if not built-in)
Cabinet, storage	1 per room
* Chair, easy	2 per room
Chair, desk	1 per desk
Chair, general purpose	4 per room
Desk	1 per room (when not in bedroom)
Lamp, floor	1 per room
* Lamp, table	1 per night table and occasional table
Lamp, desk	1 per desk
Mirror, framed	1 per room
Pictures, framed	2 per room
Refrigerator	1 per room
* Rug	Reasonable coverage
* Rug pad	1 per rug (over 3 by 6 ft)
* Sofa	1 per room (when not in bedroom)
* Table, coffee	1 per room
Table, general purpose	1 per room
* Table, occasional	2 per room
* Wastebasket	1 per room

5. <u>Allowances for BOQ, Transient Officer Housing:</u> Combination Living/Dining Room. The allowance for a combination living/dining room is the same as that for living room suite, except that one dining table can be substituted for one general purpose table; and one buffet or china cabinet may be added per room. A refrigerator is not allowed. This applies to a living/dining room for single or joint use with a fully equipped common area kitchen.

6. <u>Allowances for BOQ, Transient Officer Housing</u>: Combination Living Room/Bedroom Without a Kitchen

Item	Basis of Issue
* Bed	1 per room
* Blanket	1 per bed (up to 2 additional blankets in cold climates)
Bookcase	1 per room (if not built-in)
Cabinet, storage	1 per room
* Chair, desk	1 per desk
Chair, easy	2 per individual
Chair, general purpose	4 per room
* Desk	1 per room
* Dresser or Chest of Drawers	1 per room
Lamp, floor	1 per room
* Lamp, table	1 per night table and occasional table
Lamp, desk	1 per desk
Mattress Pad	1 per bed
Mirror, framed	1 per dresser or chest of drawers
* Mirror, full length	1 per room or suite
* Picture, framed	2 per room
* Pillow, bed	1 per bed
* Pillowcase	2 per pillow
* Refrigerator	1 per room or suite
* Rug	Reasonable coverage
* Rug pad	1 per rug (over 3 by 6 ft)
Rack, luggage	1 per bed (in transient quarters)
* Sheet, bed	4 per bed
* Sofa	1 per room (in lieu of easy chair, space permitting)
* Table, coffee	1 per room
Table, general purpose	1 per room
* Table, occasional	1 per room
* Wardrobe	1 per individual (when not built in) (Additional storage may be authorized to meet special requirements.)
* Wastebasket	1 per room
* Wastebasket	1 per bathroom

7. <u>Allowances for BOQ, Transient Officer Housing: Combination Living Room/Bedroom With Kitchen</u>. The allowance for a combination living/bedroom with fully equipped kitchen is the same as that for a combination living/bedroom without kitchen facilities except as follows:

a. Additions. Add the following:

Item	Basis of Issue
Chair, dining	4 per room
Table, dining	1 per room
Buffet or China Cabinet	1 per room

b. Deletions. Delete the following:

Item	Basis of Issue
Refrigerator	1 per room or suite

8. Allowances for BOQ Residential-Type Living Room. Same as Suite - living room (without kitchen facilities).

9. Allowances for BOQ Residential-Type Combination Living/Dining Room. Same as combination living/dining room (with kitchen facility), except six dining chairs are permitted.

10. Allowances for BOQ Lounge. The allowance for a BOQ lounge is the same as that for a BEQ lounge.(2)

(2) Lounges in multi floor BEQ/BOQ may be designated for a specific purpose such as TV room, game room, athletic areas, or reading room.

GARRISON PROPERTY POLICY MANUAL
APPENDIX E
TABLE OF ALLOWANCES--OFFICE FURNITURE

Item	Flag/SES Level (Class A)	Col/GM-15 Level (Class A)	LtCol/Major GM-13/14 Level (Class B)	Captain & Below E9 & Below GS-1 to GS-12 Level (Class C)
Bookcase	1	1	1	--
Chair, easy	2(a)/	1(a)/	--	--
Chair, rotary desk	1	1	1	1
Chair, side w/arms	6(a)/	6(a)	3(b)/	1
Chair, side w/o arms	3	--	--	3(b)/
Costumer	1	1	--	(c)/
Credenza	1	1	(d)/	(e)/
Desk, double pedestal, conference	1	--	--	--
Desk, double pedestal, flat top	--	1	1	1(e)/
Sofa	1(a)/	1(a)/	--	--
Table:				
Conference 72 x 36 in	1(a)/	--	--	--
Conference 60 x 30 in	--	1(a)/	--	--
Conference 40 x 30 in	--	--	1(b)/	1(b)/
Table, coffee	1(a)/	1(a)/	--	--
Table, end				
Telephone stand	1	1	--	--
Workstation	--	--	--	(c)/
Workstation, executive				
VDT, L-Unit	(f)/	--	(d)/	--

(a)/ Choice of conference table and chairs, or sofa and easy chair for deputy positions

(b)/ For supervisory positions

(c)/ As required

(d)/ Choice of one

(e)/ For supervisory positions in private offices

(f)/ As required for Executive Support Staff

TYPICAL WORKSTATION LAYOUT

Manager Open Office - 01:

The 01 System configuration (110 ft(2) with aisle space), a U-shaped workspace will accommodate a chair, 2-3 side chairs, a computer and printer, open work space and convergent worksurface (to accommodate conferences), mobile locking pedestals (2) for working files, overhead storage with flipper doors, and open overhead storage area for reference materials.(1)

For planning purposes, the overhead storage areas with flipper doors are each 30 in long, 15 in wide and 14 in high. The 90o corner unit is equipped with an adjustable sliding keyboard shelf. The work surfaces permit electric, telephone or data cable connection. Under shelf lighting is available to supplement ceiling lighting.

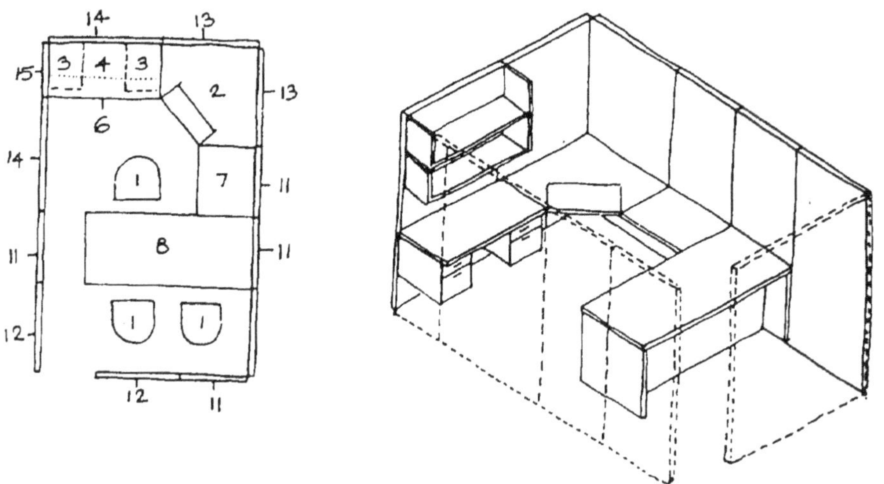

---

(1) See Workstation Component List for actual parts.

TYPICAL WORKSTATION LAYOUT

Professional Workstation - 02:

The 02 System configuration (90 ft(2) with aisle space), a U-shaped workspace, will accommodate a chair and side chair, a computer and printer, open work area, mobile locking pedestals for working files (2), overhead storage with flipper doors (2) for files and an open overhead storage area for reference materials.(1)

For planning purposes, the overhead storage areas with flipper doors are each 30 in long, 15 in wide and 15 in high. The 90 degree corner unit is equipped with an adjustable sliding keyboard shelf. The worksurfaces permit electric, telephone or data cable connection. Under shelf lighting is available to supplement ceiling lighting.

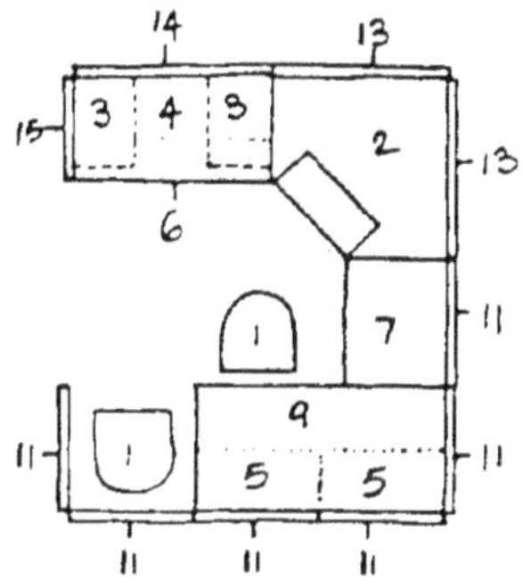

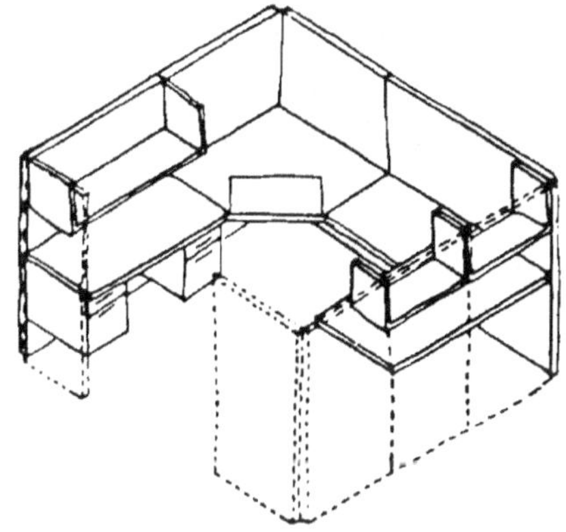

(1) See Workstation Component List for actual parts.

TYPICAL WORKSTATION LAYOUT

Clerical Workstation - O3:

The O3 System configuration (60 ft(2) with aisle space), an L-shaped workspace will accommodate a chair, a computer and printer, an open work area and a mobile locking pedestal.(1)

For planning purposes, the 6 ft work surface is equipped with an adjustable keyboard shelf. The 4 ft. work area is adjacent to, and lower than, the keyboard work area. All worksurfaces permit electric, telephone or data cable connection. The pedestal is equipped for pencils and file storage.

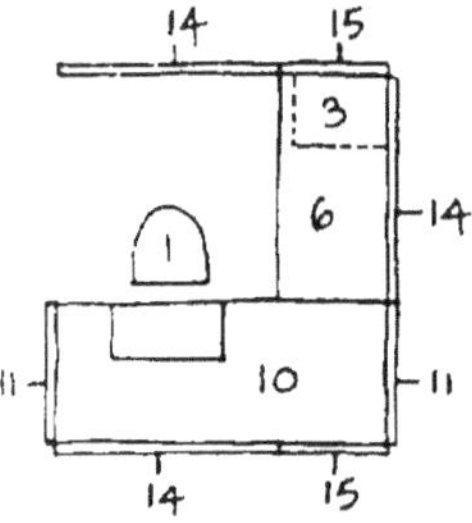

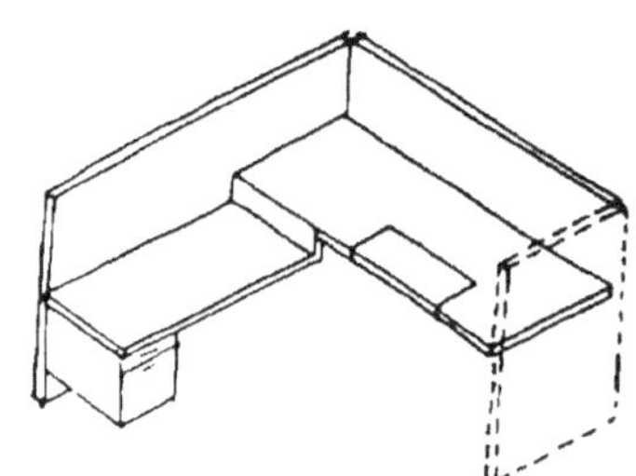

Reception Area Workstation -O3R:

The O3 System configuration will be the same as the O3, but with a 4 ft high counter. A ledge area will be around the workstation perimeter for visitor reception.

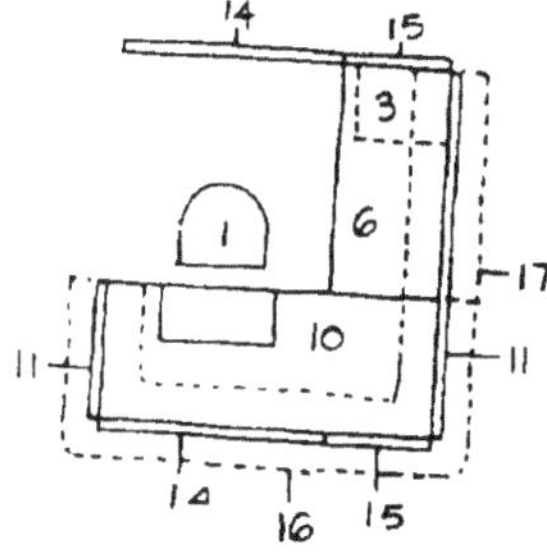

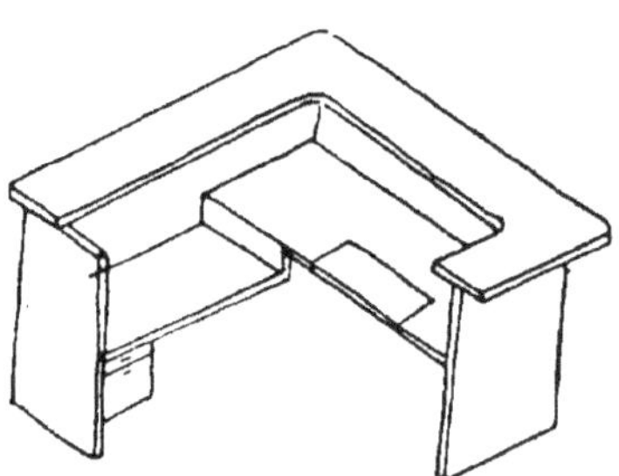

(1) See Workstation Component List for actual parts.

WORKSTATION COMPONENT LIST

1 Chair

2 Corner Unit w/Keyboard Shelf (90o)

3 Drawer Pedestal (1 ft 3 in x 1 ft 10 in x 1 ft 6 in)

4 Open Shelf (4 ft x 1 ft 3 in x 1 ft 3 in)

5 Open Shelf (2 ft 6 in x 1 ft 3 in x 1 ft 3 in)

6 Work Surface (4 ft x 2 ft x 1 1/2 in)

7 Work Surface (2 ft 6 in x 2 ft x 1 1/2 in)

8 Work Surface (6 ft x 2 ft 6 in x 1 1/2 in)

9 Work Surface (5 ft x 2 ft 6 in x 1 1/2 in)

10 Work Surface w/Keyboard Shelf (6 ft x 2 ft 6 in x 1 1/2 in)

11 Panel (2 ft 6 in Wide)

12 Panel (3 ft 0 in Wide)

13 Panel (3 ft 6 in Wide)

14 Panel (4 ft 0 in Wide)

15 Panel (2 ft 0 in Wide)

16 Ledge (1 ft 3 in Deep)

17 Straight Ledge

Notes: 1. All panels are 2 1/2 inches thick.

2. Panels at Office O-1 are 6 ft 8 in high.

3. Panels at Office O-2 are 5 ft 0 in high.

4. Panels at Office O-3 are 4 ft 0 in high.

GARRISON PROPERTY POLICY MANUAL

APPENDIX F

MINIMUM STANDARDS OF ADEQUACY

1. PERMANENT PARTY PERSONNEL AND PERMANENT CHANGE OF STATION (PCS) STUDENTS

a. Officer Personnel

Grade	Net Living Area Per Person	Accommodations
O-3 and above	400 ft(2) (36 m(2))	Private quarters consisting of living room, bedroom, private bath with access to kitchen, or officers dining facility receiving appropriated fund support.
O-1, O-2, and all warrant officers	250 ft(2) (22.5 m(2))	Private quarters consisting of sleeping/living room and private bath.

b. Enlisted Personnel

Grade	Net Living Area Per Person	Accommodations
E-6 through E-9	270 ft(2) (24.3 m(2))	Private room with bath rooms.
E-5	135 ft(2) (8.1 m(2))	No more than two to a room, bath shared with not more than one other person.
E-1 to E-4	72 ft(2) (6.48 m(2))	No more than four to a room central head facilities.
E-1 (recruits, trainees, and "A" school students)	72 ft(2) (6.48 m(2))	Open bay, central head facilities.

2. TEMPORARY DUTY/TRANSIENT PERSONNEL

a. Officer Personnel

Grade	Net Living Area Per Person	Accommodations
All officers, warrant officers, and all civilians	250 ft(2) (22.5 m(2))	Private room, shared bath with no more than one other person.

b. Enlisted Personnel

Grade	Net Living Area Per Person	Accommodations
E-6 through E-9	250 ft(2) (22.5 m(2))	Private room, bath shared with no more than one other person.
E-5	135 ft(2) (12.15 m(2))	No more than two to a room, bath shared with no more than one other person.
E-1 through E-4	90 ft(2) (8.1 m(2))	No more than four to a room, central head facilities.
E-1 (recruits, trainees, and "A" school students)	72 ft(2) (6.48 m(2))	Open bay, central head facilities.

TYPICAL BEQ LAYOUT 1

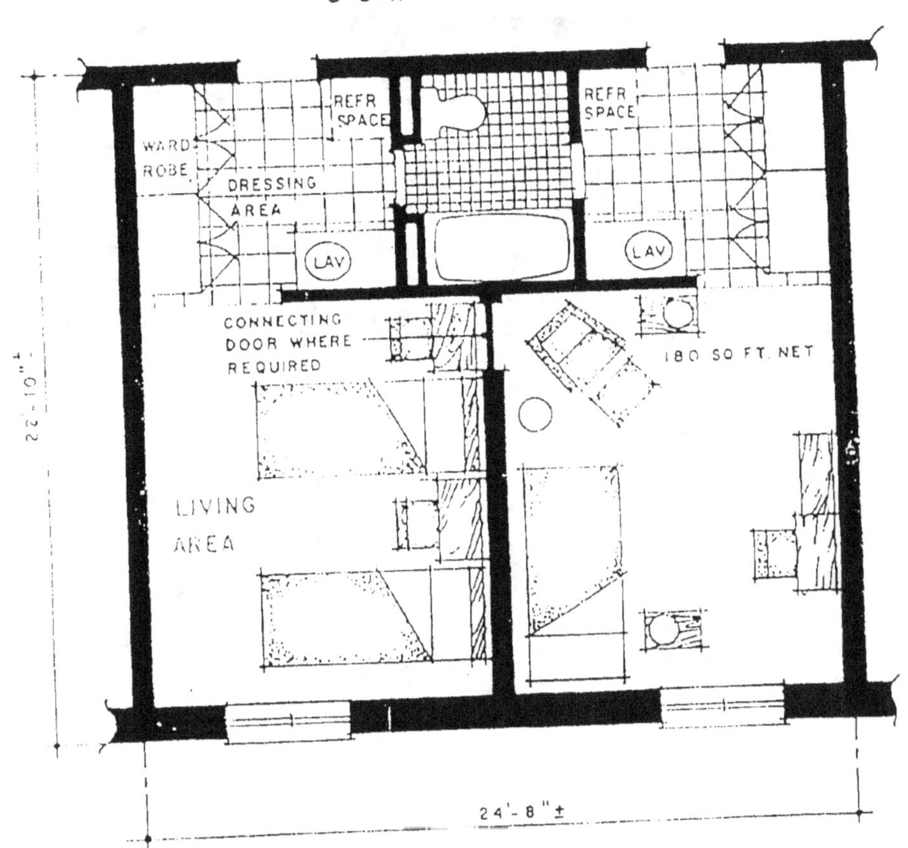

[1] BEQ layout for interior corridor type rooms.

TYPICAL BEQ LAYOUT 2

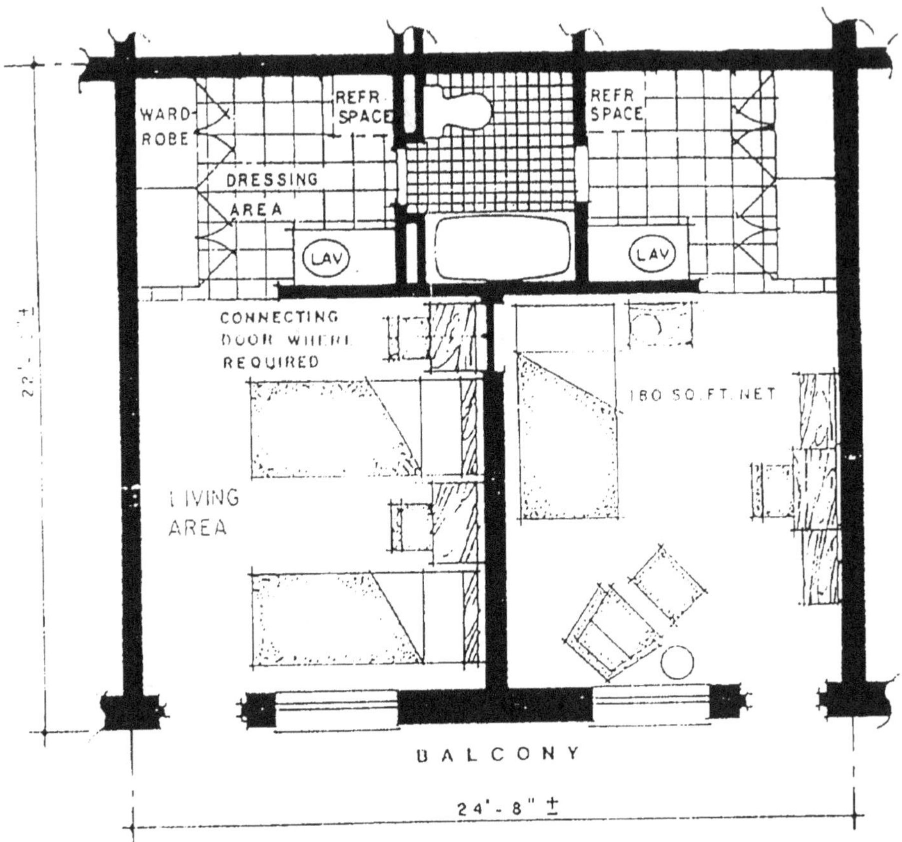

(2) BEQ layout for balcony type rooms.

PRIVATE QUARTERS 3

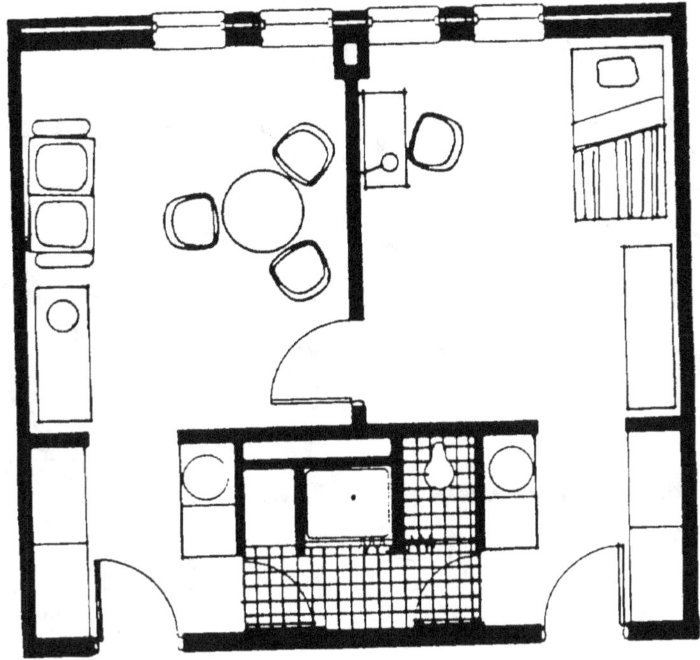

---

(3) Quarters consist of sleeping and living area and private bath.

TYPICAL COMMUNITY USE AREAS 4

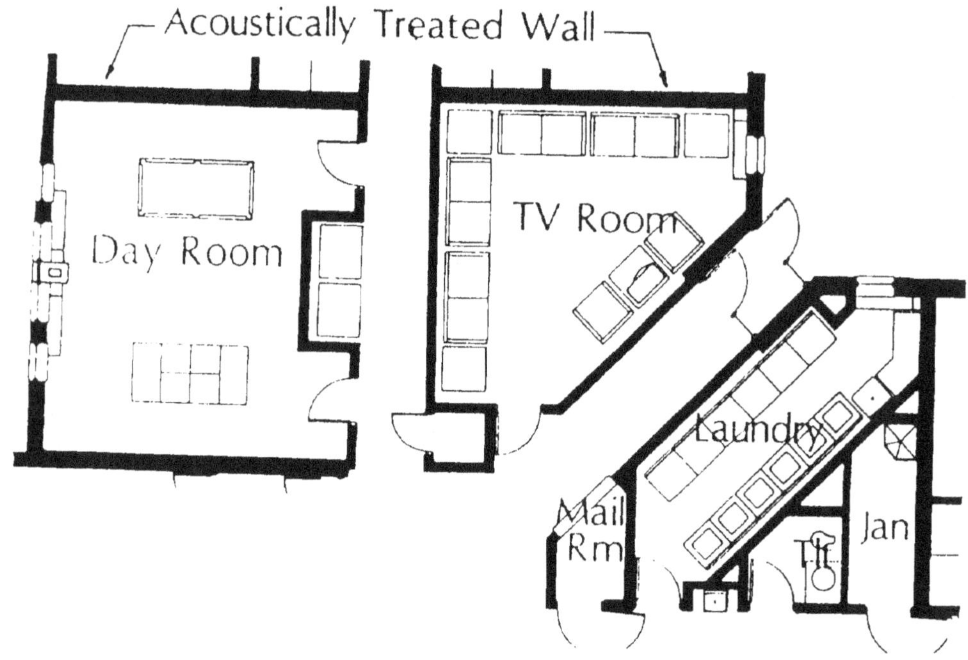

---

(4) Community room layout for dayroom with ping-pong or pool table or TV room. Laundry room based on one washer and dryer per 17 persons.

1. Supply Codes

Code	Title	Remarks
A	Serviceable Without Qualification	New, unused, or reconditioned material that is serviceable and issuable to all customers without limitation or restriction. Includes material with more than 6 months shelf-life remaining.
B	Serviceable With Qualification	New, used, repaired, or reconditioned material that is serviceable and issuable for its intended purpose but which is restricted from issue to specific units, activities, or geographical areas because of its limited usefulness or short life expectancy. Includes material with 3 to 6 months shelf-life remaining.
C	Serviceable (Priority Item)	Items that are serviceable and issuable to selected customers, but that must be issued before condition codes A and B and B material with less than 3 months shelf life remaining.
D	Serviceable (Test/Modification)	Serviceable material that requires test, alteration, modification, conversion, or disassembly. This does not include items that must be inspected or tested immediately prior to issue.
E	Unserviceable (Limited Repair)	Material that involves only limited expense or restore to serviceable condition and that is accomplished in the storage activity where the stock is located.
F	Unserviceable (Reparable)	Economically reparable material that requires repair, overhaul, or reconditioning. This includes reparable items that are radioactively contaminated.
G	Unserviceable (Incomplete)	Material requiring additional parts components to complete the end item prior to issue.

Code	Title	Remarks
H	Unserviceable (Condemned)	Material that has been determined to be unserviceable and does not meet repair criteria. This includes condemned items that are radioactively contaminated.
S	Unserviceable (Scrap)	Material that has no value except for basic material content. No stock will be recorded as on hand in condition code S. This code is used only on transactions involving shipments to the DRMO's. Material will not be transferred to condition code S prior to turn in to the DRMO, if material is recorded in condition codes A through H at the time the material is determined excess. Material identified by NSN will not be identified by this condition code.

2. DISPOSAL CONDITION CODES

Code	Title	Remarks
1	Unused - Good	Unused property that is usable without repairs and identical or interchangeable with new items from normal supply source.
2	Unused - Fair	Unused property that is usable without repairs, but is deteriorated or damaged to the extent that utility is somewhat impaired.
3	Unused - Poor	Unused property that is without repairs, but is considerably deteriorated or damaged. Enough utility remains to classify the property better than salvage.
4	Used - Good	Used property that is usable without repairs and most of its useful life remains.
5	Used - Fair	Used property that is usable without repairs, but is somewhat worn or deteriorated and may soon require repairs.

Code	Title	Remarks
6	Used - Poor	Used property that may be used without repairs, but is considerably worn or deteriorated to the degree that remaining utility is limited or major repairs will soon be required.
7	Repairs Required - Good	Required repairs are minor and should not exceed 15 percent of original acquisition cost.
8	Repairs Required - Fair	Required repairs are considerable and are estimated to range from 16 percent to 40 percent of original acquisition cost.
9	Repairs Required -	Required repairs are major because the property is badly aged, worn, or deteriorated and are estimated to range from 41 percent to 65 percent of original acquisition cost.
X	Salvage	Property has some value in excess of its basic material content, but repair or rehabilitation to use for the originally intended purpose is clearly impractical. Repair for any use would exceed 65 percent of the original acquisition cost.
S	Scrap	Material that has no value except for its basic material content.

APPENDIX H

TABLE OF AUTHORIZED MATERIAL CONTROL NUMBERS

1. Equipment Category: HL120-HL210
   (LSN's: 7010-00-vvv-D001/D999) (1/)

2. Central Processing Unit (CPU): HL120-129
   (LSN's: 7010-00-vvv-D001/D020 and 7010-00-vvv-D501/D600)

   a. Table Model

      (1) Tempest (Certified for Tempest Maintenance): HL125

      (2) Nontempest: HL124

   b. Portable Model

      (1) Tempest (Certified for Tempest Maintenance:) HL127

      (2) Nontempest: HL126

   c. Lap Model: HL128

3. Monitors (Color/Monochrome): HL130-139
   (LSN's: 7010-00-vvv-D030/D039 and 7010-00-vvv-D601/D700)

4. Printers: HL140-149
   (LSN's: 7010-00-vvv-D040/D059 and 7010-00-vvv-D701/D800)

   a. Dot Matrix

      (1) Tempest (Certified for Tempest Maint.): HL141

      (2) Nontempest: HL140

   b. Letter Quality

      (1) Tempest (Certified for Tempest Maint.): HL142

      (2) Nontempest: HL143

5. Disk Drives: HL150-159
   (LSN's: 7010-00-vvv-D060/D079)

   a. Floppy Disk Drive: HL150-153

   b. Non-Removable Hard Disk Drive: HL154-156

   c. Removable Hard: HL157-159

6. Software: HL160-169
(LSN's: 7010-00-vvv-D150/D200 and 7010-00-vvv-D801/D900)

7. Graphics Plotters: HL170-179
(LSN's: 7010-00-vvv-D080/D089)

a. (1) Tempest (Certified for Tempest Maintenance): HL170

(2) Nontempest: HL171

b. Graphics Tablet

(1) Tempest (Certified for Tempest Maintenance): HL172

(2) Nontempest: HL173

8. Networking ADPE (LAN): HL180-189
(LSN's: 7010-00-vvv-D090/D099)

a. Lines

(1) Tempest (Certified for Tempest Maintenance): HL180

(2) Nontempest: HL181

b. Modems

(1) Tempest (Certified for Tempest Maintenance): HL182

(2) Nontempest: HL183

9. Miscellaneous Peripheral Equipment (Other): HL190-210
(LSN's: 7010-00-vvv-D100/D149 and 7010-00-vvv-D901/D999)

a. Paper Tape Media (Nontempest): HL190

b. Magnetic Tape Unit: HL191

c. Word Processor

(1) Tempest (Certified for Tempest Maintenance): HL192

(2) Nontempest: HL193

d. Communications Server

(1) Tempest (Certified for Tempest Maintenance): HL194

(2) Nontempest: HL195

e. Media Access Unit

(1) Tempest (Certified for Tempest Maintenance): HL196

(2) Nontempest: HL197

f. Additional Equipment: HL198-HL210

(1/)vvv = Variable according to assigned unit

APPENDIX I

MINOR PROPERTY IDENTIFICATION CODES

Command	Serial Number Range				
1st MCD	1D	0000000001	-	1D	9999999999
12th MCD	2D	0000000001	-	2D	9999999999
4th MCD	4D	0000000001	-	4D	9999999999
6th MCD	6D	0000000001	-	6D	9999999999
8th MCD	8D	0000000001	-	8D	9999999999
MB 8th & I	8I	0000000001	-	8I	9999999999
9th MCD	9D	0000000001	-	9D	9999999999
Albany	AL	0000000001	-	AL	9999999999
MATSC MS	AT	0000000001	-	AT	9999999999
Barstow	BA	0000000001	-	BA	9999999999
Beaufort	BE	0000000001	-	BE	9999999999
Camp Butler	CB	0000000001	-	CB	9999999999
Camp Elmore	CE	0000000001	-	CE	9999999999
Cherry Point	CH	0000000001	-	CH	9999999999
Camp Lejeune	CL	0000000001	-	CL	9999999999
Camp Pendleton	CP	0000000001	-	CP	9999999999
Camp Smith	CS	0000000001	-	CS	9999999999
El Toro	ET	0000000001	-	ET	9999999999
MCSA, KC	FC	0000000001	-	FC	9999999999
HqBn, Henderson Hall	HH	0000000001	-	HH	9999999999
HQMC	HQ	0000000001	-	HQ	9999999999
Iwakuni	IW	0000000001	-	IW	9999999999
Kaneohe Bay	KB	0000000001	-	KB	9999999999
FMFLant, Norfolk	LA	0000000001	-	LA	9999999999
LFTC, Little Creek	LC	0000000001	-	LC	9999999999
New River	NR	0000000001	-	NR	9999999999
FMFPac	PA	0000000001	-	PA	9999999999
Parris Island	PI	0000000001	-	PI	9999999999
Quantico	QU	0000000001	-	QU	9999999999
MCRSC	RC	0000000001	-	RC	9999999999
4th MarDiv	RD	0000000001	-	RD	9999999999
4th MAW	RW	0000000001	-	RW	9999999999
San Diego	SD	0000000001	-	SD	9999999999
MATSG TN	TN	0000000001	-	TN	9999999999
Twentynine Palms	TP	0000000001	-	TP	9999999999
Tustin	TU	0000000001	-	TU	9999999999
MATSG TX	TX	0000000001	-	TX	9999999999
Yuma	YU	0000000001	-	YU	9999999999

APPENDIX J

LIFE EXPECTANCIES

1. PSE

Item	Years
Bed	10
Bureau	10
Chair: Dining	6
Chair: Desk	10
Curtains and Drapes	5-7
Desk	10
Dryers, Clothes	3
Icemaking Machines	6
Ranges (Cooking Stoves)	8
Refrigerators (5.5 Cu Ft.)	10
Secretary (Desk/Wall unit)	10
Table: Dining	6
Table: Coffee, End, Night	10
Washers, Clothes	3

2. FPSE

Item	Years
Bread Slicing Machine	8
Cabinet: Dough Proofing	10
Cabinet: Food Warmer, Pass through	8
Cabinet: Warmer, Roll	16
Charbroiler: Gas and Electric	6
Cash Register: Electronic	6
Coffee Maker: Automatic Vacuum 465BB	6
Coffee Maker Set: Vacuum, Upper and Lower Bowls	6
Cold Food Counter, Refrigerator	8
Compactor: Refuse	8
Conveyor Belt Driven	12
Cooker: Steam or Electric, Self-Generating	8
Dishwashing Machine	10
Dishwashing Machine, Commercial, Continuous Oval	10
Dispenser: Bread, Sliced, Compartment	5
Dispenser: Drinking Water, Mechanically Cooled	10
Dispenser: Ice Tea	6
Dispenser: Juice, 4-Gallon Capacity	6
Dispenser: Juice, 13-Gallon Capacity	6
Dispenser: Milk, Refrigerator, 5-Gallon Capacity	10
Dispenser: Milk, Refrigerator, 10-Gallon Capacity	10
Dispenser: Tableware	6
Dough: Mixing Machine	8
Dough: Molding Machine, Loaf	8
Dough: Rolling Machine, Pie	8
Doughnut Machine: Cutting and Frying, Electric	8
Flour Handling Plant	8
Food Container: Warmer, ICTP-33-H	6

Item	Years
Food Cutter Machine: Electric	8
Food Warmer: Infrared	6
Frozen Food Cabinet: Mech., Reach-In, 18 to 22 ft(3)	8
Fryers: Deep Fat, Electric or Gas	8
Griddle: Self-Heating	6
Grinder: Meat, Electric	8
Hot Plate: Electric, 4 Heating Units	4
Ice Cream Cabinet: Mechanical, Refrigerator	10
Ice Cream Plant: 1-1/2-Gallon per Batch	8
Ice Cream Plant: Portable	12
Icemaking Machine: Flake, 275 lb per 24 hours, Counter Type	6
Icemaking Machine: Cube, 500 lb per 24 hours	8
Icemaking Machine: Flake, 1,000 lb per 24 hours	8
Kettles: Steam, Gas, Electric, Mounted on Legs	8
Machine: Washing, Pots and Pans	6
Meat: Slicing Machine, Electric	6
Meat: Tenderizer, Electric	6
Mixer: Fluid, Electric (AD-DC)	6
Mixing Machine: Food, Electric	8
Moulding Machine: Meat, Fish	8
Opener: Can, Electric	5
Oven: Baking, Electric, Gas, Mixed Gas, Liquefied Petroleum	6
Oven: Convection	8
Oven: Microwave	8
Pan: Frying, Tilting	10
Preflushing Machine	8
Range: Electric or Gas	10
Refrigerator: Mech., Comm., Pass Through, 65 ft(3)	8
Refrigerator: Mech, Comm, Reach-In, 65 ft(3)	8
Refrigerator: Mech, Household, 12.5 ft(3)	5
Refrigerator: Mech, Pass Through, 40 ft(3)	8
Refrigerator: Prefab., 600 ft(3)	12
Refrigerator: Reach-In, 20 ft(3)	8
Refrigerator: Unit, Mech., 10,000 BTU	8
Refrigerator: Walk-In, 150 ft(3)	8
Rinser: Sterilizer, Electric	8
Sandwich Unit: Refrigerator	8
Sandwich Wrapping Machine	6
Sifting Machine: Flour, Electric	10
Saw: Bank, Meat Cutting	8
Soft Ice Cream Maker	6
Table: Hot Food, Gas, Electric, Steam	8
Table: Food Preparation	10
Toaster: Gas or Electric	6
Toaster: Electric Pop-Up	3
Truck: Storing and Transportation	12
Urn: Coffee, Gas, Steam, Electric	8
Vegetable Cutter	8
Vegetable Peeling Machine	8
Waffle Iron: Electric	5

APPENDIX K

SAMPLE MINOR PROPERTY ITEM (1)

Aerifier
Air Compressor
Asphalt Cutter
Asphalt Kettle
Battery Charger
Bush Hog
Calculator
Check Signer
Conveyor
Copying Machine
Disc Rooter
Drill
Embosser
Floor Jointer
Fogger Unit
Generator
Grinding Machine
Hoist
Imprinter
Insecticide Sprayer
Lathe
Lawn Mower,
  Gang
  Rotary
  Self-Propelled (Less than 30 Drawbar HP)
  Sickle-towed
Log Splitter
Microfiche Reader/Printer
Mixer, Portable Concrete
Mulch Spreader
Musical Instruments
Paint Sprayer
Paper Cutter
Portable Radio
Power Jack
Printer
Pump,
  Centrifugal
  Diaphragm
  Sump
Rotary Tiller
Sander Attachment
Saw
Saw, Concrete
Seed Planter
Sewer Rodder
Sewing Machine
Snow Plow
Sod Cutter
Sprayer,
  Aerosol
  Agriculture
  Cleaner
  Duster
Sweeper,
  Lawn
  Drawn
Stream Cleaner
Stencil Cutting Machine
Tape Recorder
Tire Changer
Tools
Typewriter
Welder

---

(1) The above illustrates typical minor property items, but is not all inclusive. Similar property may be plant property dependent on acquisition cost. See chapter 6 for budget information.

APPENDIX L

FORMS AND INSTRUCTIONS

This appendix contains the following forms and their instructions:

GARRISON PROPERTY
BUDGET AND REPORT REQUIREMENTS
SCHEDULE

Due Date		Submit
Jan	02	Begin Plant Account (PA) Inventory
	10	CSE PMC Status Report
	18	NavCompt 167 Report
	31	FPSE O&M Budget
	31	Minor Property O&M Budget
Feb	28	Complete Plant Account Inventory
Mar	15	MCON CE Project Requirements
	15	MFIP Project Requirements
Apr	10	CSE PMC Status Report
	15	Plant Account Report
	18	NavCompt 167 Report
Jul	1	Begin ADPE Inventory
	1	Begin PSE Inventory
	10	CSE PMC Status Report(1)
	10	Warehouse Modernization Requirements
	18	NavCompt 167 Report
Aug	15	Complete ADPE Inventory
	31	Complete PSE Inventory
Sep	15	PSE Inventory Report
Oct	10	CSE PMC Status Report
	15	Plant Account Report
	18	NavCompt 167 Report
Nov	30	CSE PMC Aggregate Budget

(1) Include each prioritized line item requirement for the next fiscal year.

INSTRUCTIONS FOR:

INVENTORY, REQUIREMENTS, BUDGET, AND REPLACEMENT (IRBAR) PLAN

1. Number of Buildings. Enter the number of buildings that represent the number of individual structures comprising the BEQ/BOQ. For messhalls or administrative offices enter the number of structures.

2. BEQ/BOQ Capacity. BEQ/BOQ capacity is a cumulative figure representing the number of personnel the station plans to accommodate. Enter the total capacity in number of beds (e.g., a BEQ/BOQ has 100 rooms; 74 rooms are equipped with 1 bed and 13 two-room suites are equipped with 1 bed; therefore, the total capacity is 87 (74 plus 13) and not 100).

3. Activity. Enter the activity completing the form.

4. Date. Enter the date.

5. Item Description. Enter a description of the item.

6. Total Inventory. The total inventory reflects PSE items currently in the BEQ/BOQ and includes the purchase price for each item. Items in disposal condition should not be included, but on-hand reparable PSE items should be included.

7. Inventory Condition. Enter the inventory condition using the codes in appendix G.

8. Total Requirements. Enter the requirements for repair, augmentation, or replacement.

9. Shortfall Total. Enter the deficiencies, including prior year unfunded deficiencies.

10. Projected Replacement. Enter the planned replacement for the next fiscal year and replacement requirement for the next 2 fiscal years.

    a. Fiscal Year.

    b. Expected Total.

    c. Fiscal Year.

    d. Expected Total.

    e. Fiscal Year.

    f. Expected Total.

GARRISON PROPERTY POLICY MANUAL

(RCS EXEMPT)

FOOD PREPARATION AND SERVING EQUIPMENT (FPSE) REQUIREMENTS FOR MESSHALLS

ACTIVITY: ____________________ POC: ____________________

AUTOVON NO.: ____________________

	Item Priority	Item Description (NSN)	Replace Plant Acct/Serial No.	Quantity New Procurement	Quantity Replacement	Cost New Procurement	Cost Replacement	Total Cost
1.								
2.								
3.								
4.								
5.								
6.								
7.								
8.								
9.								

L-5

INSTRUCTIONS FOR:
FOOD PREPARATION AND SERVING EQUIPMENT (FPSE) REQUIREMENTS
FOR MESSHALLS

REPORT CONTROL SYMBOL (EXEMPT)

1. Fiscal Year. Enter the fiscal year for which the requirement is budgeted.

2. Activity. Enter the activity address code.

3. POC. Provide a point of contact familiar with the equipment requirements.

4. Defense Switched Network. Provide a telephone number for the point of contact.

5. Item Priority. Prioritize each item in the desired order for procurement.

6. Item Description. Enter a noun description and national stock number (NSN) for each type of equipment.

7. Replace Plant Acct/Serial No. Enter the plant account number if item will replace existing plant account property.

8. Quantity New Procurement. Enter the quantity if the item is for new procurement.

9. Quantity Replacement. Enter the quantity if the item will replace existing plant account property.

10. Cost New Procurement. Enter the unit cost if the item is for new procurement.

11. Cost Replacement. Enter the unit cost if the item will replace existing plant account property.

12. Total Cost. Enter the total cost on each page and a summary of total costs on the last page of multiple pages.

13. Totals. Enter the total cost on each page and a summary of total costs on the last page.

REPORT CONTROL SYMBOL (EXEMPT)

MESSHALL FACILITY IMPROVEMENT PROGRAM (MFIP) BUDGET
FISCAL YEAR 19_

ACTIVITY: ____________________ POC: ______________

DSN NO: __________________

BUDGET YEAR + 1:
MFIP PROJECT NO: ____________ FY _______________

MESSHALL/LOCATION: ____________ FY LAST UPGRADED: _____

VALIDATED: YES____NO____APPROVED: YES____NO____

A&E STATUS: _________________ A&E FUNDS REQUIRED: __

FUNDS CATEGORY: AMOUNT: ____________

A. MINOR CONSTRUCTION OR REPAIR: __________

B. EXPENSE EQUIPMENT: __________

C. INVESTMENT EQUIPMENT __________

D. DECOR PACKAGE: __________

E. INSTALLATION COSTS: __________

TOTAL FUNDS REQUIRED: __________

FUNDS CATEGORY DESCRIPTION:
A. MINOR CONSTRUCTION OR REPAIR: (Scope & Built-in Equipment)

B. EXPENSE EQUIPMENT: (List FPSE Equipment)

C. INVESTMENT EQUIPMENT: (List CSE Food Service Equipment)

D. DECOR PACKAGE: (List Theme Motif; Furniture and Accessories)

E. INSTALLATION COSTS: (Expense Equipment)

BUDGET YEAR + 2
MFIP PROJECT NO: ____________ FY _______________

MESSHALL/LOCATION:____________ FY LAST UPGRADED: ____

VALIDATED: YES ____NO ____APPROVED: YES ____NO____

A&E STATUS: _________________ A&E FUNDS REQUESTED: __

FUNDS CATEGORY: AMOUNT:
A. MINOR CONSTRUCTION OR REPAIR: __________

B. EXPENSE EQUIPMENT: __________

C. INVESTMENT EQUIPMENT: __________

D. DECOR PACKAGE: __________

E. INSTALLATION COSTS: __________

TOTAL FUNDS REQUIRED: __________

A. MINOR CONSTRUCTION OR REPAIR: (Scope & Built-in Equipment)

B. EXPENSE EQUIPMENT: (List FPSE Equipment)

C. INVESTMENT EQUIPMENT: (List CSE Food Service Equipment)

D. DECOR PACKAGE: (List Theme Motif; Furniture and Accessories)

E. INSTALLATION COSTS: (Expense Equipment)

INSTRUCTIONS FOR:

MESSHALL FACILITY IMPROVEMENT PROGRAM (MFIP) BUDGET
REPORT CONTROL SYMBOL (EXEMPT)

1. Fiscal Year. Enter the current fiscal year the budget is prepared.

2. Activity. Enter the reporting command authorized funds.

3. POC. Enter the activity point of contact for the MFIP program.

4. DSN NO. Enter the DSN telephone number for the POC.

5. Budget Year + 1. Identify projects for the next budget year. (Prepare a separate budget for each project in each fiscal year.)

6. MFIP Project No. Enter the project number of the activity assigned for each project.

7. FY. Enter scheduled fiscal year for contract award of the project.

8. Messhall/Location. Enter the name and number used to to identify the messhall facility.

9. FY Last Upgraded. Provide specific geographical area where facility is located.

10. Validated. Indicate if CMC (LFF) has validated and approved the project, as "yes" or "no."

11. Approved. Indicate if A&E design documentation was approved at command level as "yes"or "no."

12. A&E Status. Indicate percent of architectural and engineering (A&E) design completed.

13. A&E Funds Requested. Indicate funds required to perform the A&E design efforts for the project.

14. Funds Category. Indicate funds required for each category.

a. Minor Construction. Indicate amount required for repair or construction costs and any built-in or installed equipment.

b. Expense Equipment. Indicate O&M amount required to procure FPSE items.

c. Investment Equipment. Indicate PMC amount required to procure food service equipment. Cost should include contractor installation costs.

d. Decor Package. Indicate O&M amount required to procure new messhall furniture and accessories.

e. Installation Costs. Indicate O&M amount required to install Government- or Contractor-furnished FPSE items.

f. Total Funds Required. Total amounts listed in a through e.

15. Funds Category Description. Describe work required in each category.

a. Minor Construction. Provide general scope of work included in repair or construction phase of project and describe built-in or installed equipment required.

b. Expense Equipment. Provide list of FPSE items for procurement with O&M funds.

c. Investment Equipment. Provide list of food service investment equipment for procurement with PMC funds.

d. Decor Package. Describe motif for renovated messhall. Provide list of new messhall furniture and accessories required.

e. Installation Costs. Indicate Government- or contractor-furnished FPSE items to be installed.

16. Budget Year +2. Provide the same information identified in numbers 5-15 above for any projects scheduled for BY + 2.

GARRISON PROPERTY POLICY MANUAL

(Report Control Symbol (Exempt))

COLLATERAL EQUIPMENT REQUIREMENTS (INITIAL OUTFITTING)					DATE	
ACTIVITY (Name, Location, UIC)						
PROJECT TITLE				PROJECT NUMBER	MCON FY	CONST BOD
COG SYMBOL AND FED STOCK NO OR OTHER SOURCE	ITEM EQUIPMENT DESCRIPTION	QUAN-TITY	UNIT OF ISSUE	UNIT PRICE	TOTAL COST	

SAMPLE

NAVFAC 4-11010/32 (4-83)

Page ______ of ______

L-10

INSTRUCTIONS FOR:
COLLATERAL EQUIPMENT REQUIREMENTS (INITIAL OUTFITTING)
REPORT CONTROL SYMBOL (EXEMPT)

1. Date. Enter the current date.

2. Activity. Enter the name and location of the activity for which the collateral equipment is required.

3. Project Title. Enter the name of the project for which the collateral equipment is required.

4. Project Number. Enter the number of the project.

5. MCON FY. Enter the fiscal year for which the project is required.

6. Construction BOD. Enter the beneficial occupancy date.

7. COG Symbol, and Federal Stock No., or Other Source. Enter furniture, furnishings, and equipment requirements, as applicable, under the headings below. This list must completely identify requirements in the following categories. A list of furniture and furnishings (noun name only) with applicable cost estimates is required. A lump-sum or per-man unit cost figure is not acceptable. If a category is not applicable, indicate N/A.

a. Built-in or Installed Equipment. Built-in or installed equipment is accessory equipment engineered and built into a facility as an integral part of the final design. Wardrobes for BEQ/BOQ and projection screens for classrooms are examples of this type of equipment. The initial costs to procure and install this equipment are specifically defined as construction costs and are included in MCON or MCNR appropriations.

b. Expense Items. Expense items are nontechnical items such as desks, beds, and chairs. Expense items, defined in chapter 6, are funded under O&MMC and O&MMCR appropriations.

c. Investment Items. Investment items are technical equipment such as cranes, copiers, and refrigerators. Investment items, defined in chapter 6, are funded under the PMC appropriation.

d. Equipment On Hand. Usable property on hand should be identified in the appropriate category, expense, or investment, with the following data provided:

(1) Total estimated replacement value of reusable equipment.

(2) Total relocation/reinstallation costs from old to new facility.

(3) Total cost of refurbishing equipment when it is economically advisable to refinish or refurbish on-hand equipment as opposed to procuring new items.

e. Equipment Funded from Other Appropriations. Funds from different appropriations or from different lines within an appropriation may be used to procure other equipment. This equipment, related directly to the operating function for which the structure is being provided, such as technical, scientific, production, and processing, should also be identified. The following are typical examples of items funded from other appropriations:

(1) Automated data processing equipment. (MCCTA-CTAR)

(2) Communications equipment. (MCCTA-CTAR)

(3) Audiovisual and photograph equipment, portable. (MCCDC-TE35)

(4) Training aids and equipment, including simulators. (MCCDC-TE35)

(5) Physical security equipment, including intrusion detection systems (IDS). (CMC - POS)

(6) GME, including forklifts. (CMC - LFS)

f. Other Expenses. Fees for transportation, crating, handling, storage, and installation for investment items should be included. The Marine Corps does not fund for contingency fees, an amount set aside for inflation or unforeseen requirements.

(1) Design cost for specialized equipment (such as camels).

(2) Storage (if necessary).

(3) Packing, crating, uncrating.

(4) Relocation (Existing equipment - usually activity funding).

g. Summary. Total expense and total investment costs.

(1) Training equipment.

(2) Technical equipment (APA, ADP, etc.).

(3) Grand total.

8. Item/Equipment Description. Enter a complete description of the item.

9. Quantity. Enter the quantity of the items described.

10. Unit of Issue. Enter a unit of issue, such as each, set, assembly.

11. Unit Price. Enter the price of the unit.

12. Total Cost. Enter the total cost of the item (unit price multiplied by quantity).

GARRISON PROPERTY POLICY MANUAL

REPORT CONTROL SYMBOL (EXEMPT)

COMMAND SUPPORT EQUIPMENT (CSE)
DETAILED PLANT EQUIPMENT ITEM EXHIBIT
(INVESTMENT EQUIPMENT)

ACTIVITY: ____________________ FISCAL YEAR: ____________________

ITEM NO.	PRIORITY	ITEM DES-CRIPTION	EQUIP. CLASS	REPLACE-MENT PA ID NO.	REPLACEMENT ITEM QTY.	REPLACEMENT ITEM UNIT PRICE	NEW PROCUREMENT QTY.	NEW PROCUREMENT UNIT PRICE	TOTAL COST

JUSTIFICATION and USER LOCATION:

(Provide Narrative)

L-13

GARRISON PROPERTY POLICY MANUAL

REPORT CONTROL SYMBOL (EXEMPT)

COMMAND SUPPORT EQUIPMENT (CSE)
DETAILED PLANT EQUIPMENT ITEM EXHIBIT
(INVESTMENT EQUIPMENT)

ACTIVITY: MCRD San Diego

FISCAL YEAR: 1994

ITEM NO.	PRIORITY	ITEM DES-CRIPTION	EQUIP. CLASS	REPLACE-MENT PA ID NO.	REPLACEMENT ITEM QTY.	REPLACEMENT ITEM UNIT PRICE	NEW PROCUREMENT QTY.	NEW PROCUREMENT UNIT PRICE	TOTAL COST
5	1	Duplexer	3 - OE	M6200406199	2	$55,000			$110,000

JUSTIFICATION and USER LOCATION:

The machine this equipment will replace is beyond economic repair. Excessive downtime is degrading turnaround time for mission essential communication and report requirements. The new equipment has faster operating capability and is less expensive to operate and maintain during the equipment life as indicated in the economic analysis completed this date. The equipment will be used in the base communications center.

COMMAND SUPPORT EQUIPMENT (CSE)
DETAILED PLANT EQUIPMENT ITEM EXHIBIT
(INVESTMENT EQUIPMENT)

ACTIVITY: MCCDC Quantico

FISCAL YEAR: 1993

ITEM NO.	PRIORITY	ITEM DES-CRIPTION	EQUIP. CLASS	REPLACE-MENT PA ID NO.	REPLACEMENT ITEM QTY.	REPLACEMENT ITEM UNIT PRICE	NEW PROCUREMENT QTY.	NEW PROCUREMENT UNIT PRICE	TOTAL COST
3	2	Milling Machine	4 - CL4				1	$85,000	$85,000

JUSTIFICATION and USER LOCATION:

The equipment has the capability to process heavy gauge metals required for facilities maintenance. The machine will provide state of the art technology and reduce production job time. The initial inquiry to DIPEC indicated the equipment is not available in the DoD inventory.

GARRISON PROPERTY POLICY MANUAL
INSTRUCTIONS FOR:
COMMAND SUPPORT EQUIPMENT (CSE) DETAILED PLANT
EQUIPMENT ITEM EXHIBIT
REPORT CONTROL SYMBOL (EXEMPT)

1. Activity. Enter the name and location of the activity for which the CSE is required.

2. Fiscal Year. Enter the fiscal year in which the requirements are submitted.

3. Item No. The activity shall assign an item number to each requirement in that fiscal year budget.

4. Priority. The activity shall prioritize each requirement according to the desired order for procurement. The activity has the flexibility to revise the priority at any time, for items not yet funded or in the procurement process.

5. Item Description. Provide a short descriptive name of item. Include the NSN, make, model, commercial item description (CID), or other identifying data.

6. Equipment Class. Enter the equipment category and plant account class.Enter class 3 for general equipment or class 4 for industrial plant equipment (IPE). Enter the equipment category, BG, OE, GP, FS, UE, or CL4. See paragraph 6005 for description of equipment category.

7. Replacement Item Plant Acct. No. Enter the PA number of plant equipment being replaced.

8. Replacement Item

(a) Qty. Enter the quantity requested to replace original equipment.

(b) Unit Price. Enter estimated unit price of item requested for replacement based on an economic analysis.

9. New Procurement

(a) Qty. Enter the quantity requested to acquire new equipment.

(b) Unit Price. Enter estimated unit price to procure new equipment based on an economic analysis.

10. Total Cost. Enter the total cost for the item or items requested.

11. Justification and User Location

a. Provide a brief justification to replace or procure the equipment. If the equipment replaces an item, indicate the condition, rationale for replacement, and benefits to be realized. For new procurements, indicate benefits to be realized. Describe the functional user and planned location for the new equipment. For class 4 equipment, indicate if DIPEC has been screened for available assets.

b. Prepare an exhibit for each requirement requested in the budget. The exhibit, economic analysis, specifications, installation requirements,and other information comprise the procurement documentation (PD).

c. Compile the data for each requirement into the activity budget for the required fiscal years. This information will be used to develop the aggregate CSE budget requirements.

REPORT CONTROL SYMBOL (EXEMPT)
COMMAND SUPPORT EQUIPMENT (CSE) BUDGET
REQUIREMENTS ($000)

ACTIVITY:

FISCAL YEAR:

CATEGORY	TYPE	CY	BY	BY+1	BY+2
BUILDING AND GROUNDS	BG	____	____	____	____
OFFICE EQUIPMENT	OE	____	____	____	____
UTILITIES EQUIPMENT	UE	____	____	____	____
GENERAL PURPOSE EQUIPMENT	GP	____	____	____	____
ENVIRONMENTAL EQUIPMENT	EN	____	____	____	____
FOOD SERVICE EQUIPMENT	FS	____	____	____	____
INDUSTRIAL PLANT EQUIPMENT (IPE)	CL4	____	____	____	____
TOTAL:		____	____	____	____

Indicate aggregate category totals from separate budget exhibits prepared for each class 3 and class 4 investment equipment requirement. Line item requirements for the next fiscal year will be submitted with the Third Quarter CSE Status Report.

INSTRUCTIONS FOR:
COMMAND SUPPORT EQUIPMENT (CSE) BUDGET REQUIREMENTS
REPORT CONTROL SYMBOL (EXEMPT)

1. Activity. Enter the name and location of the activity for which the CSE is required.

2. Fiscal Year. Enter the fiscal year in which the requirements are submitted.

3. Category. Enter the aggregate total dollar value of requirements for each category as defined in Section 6005. List FS dollar value separately from GP dollar value.

4. CY. Enter the current year for which funding is available. Enter zero if there are no requirements.

5. BY/BY + 1/BY + 2. Enter the next 3 years for which funding is required. Enter zero if there are no requirements.

6. TOTAL. Enter the total value of requirements for each column. Enter zero if there are no requirements.

RCS DN-7321 04

COMMAND SUPPORT EQUIPMENT (CSE) STATUS REPORT
(Class 3 and 4 Plant Property Type Items)

ACTIVITY: ____________________ 1.

APPN: ____________ 2.

SUBHEAD 6001 COMMAND SUPPORT EQUIPMENT 3.

CMD ACTY 4.	REF NO 5.	ITEM NOMEN 6a.	TYPE 6b.	BUDGET QTY 7a.	BUDGET COST 7b.	CURRENT ACTUAL QTY 8a.	CURRENT ACTUAL COST 8b.	OTHER/ UNDER $15,000 9.	FY FUND AUTH 10.	FY BUD REQ 11.	STAFF ACTION 12.	STAFF COMMENTS 13.	NEW PRI NO 14.	OLD PRI NO 15.	STATUS 16.	PROJECTED OBLIGATION Date 17.	APPROVED PD 18.	PROCUREMENT DOCUMENTATION (PD) ECON ANAL. 18a.	SPECS 18b.	LOG SPT PLAN 18c.	REMARKS (CNA/PA ID)* 19.

Funds Authorized $ _______________ 20.
Funds Committed $ _______________ 21.
Funds Obligated $ _______________ 22.
Funds Expended $ _______________ 23.
Funds Uncommitted $ _______________ 24.

EXAMPLE:

ACTIVITY: MCLB Barstow, CA - M62204 1.

APPN: 1791109.60012 2.

SUBHEAD 6001 COMMAND SUPPORT EQUIPMENT 3.

CMD ACTY 4.	REF NO 5.	ITEM NOMEN 6a.	TYPE 6b.	BUDGET QTY 7a.	BUDGET COST 7b.	CURRENT ACTUAL QTY 8a.	CURRENT ACTUAL COST 8b.	OTHER/ UNDER $15,000 9.	FY FUNDS AUTH. 10.	FY BUD REQ 11.	STAFF ACTION 12.	STAFF COMMEWNT 13.	NEW PRI NO 14.	OLD PRI NO 15.	STATUS 16.	PROJECTED OBLIGATION Date 17.	APPROVED PD 18.	PROCUREMENT DOCUMENTATION (PD) ECON ANAL. 18a.	SPECS 18b.	LOG SPT PLAN 18c.	REMARKS (CNA/PA ID)* 19.
Barstow	10090002	Generator	UE	1	25,000	1	27,500		91	90	LFS	APPROVED	1	2	COMMITTED	MAY 91	YES	YES	YES	YES	
Barstow	00091030	Drill Press	CL4	2	32,000	2	30,000		90	90		APPROVED	2	29	OBLIGATED	AUG 90	YES	YES	YES	SITE PREP REQD	CNA 9001-3402 Dtd Oct 24 89
Barstow	90090005	Copier, Brand	OE	2	40,000	3	60,000		90	89	AR	APPROVED	3	5	RECEIVED	JUN 90	YES	YES	YES	N/R	PA ID 62204-123456

Funds Authorized $ 175,000 _________ 20.
Funds Committed $ 171,500 _________ 21.
Funds Obligated $ 120,000 _________ 22.
Funds Expended $ 120,000 _________ 23.
Funds Uncommitted $ 3,500 _________ 24.

L-18

GARRISON PROPERTY POLICY MANUAL
COMMAND SUPPORT EQUIPMENT (CSE) STATUS REPORT
REPORT CONTROL SYMBOL DN-7321-04

STATUS REPORT GUIDELINES
COMMAND SUPPORT EQUIPMENT

(Class 3 and Class 4 Plant Property Type Items)

Data Element No./Title.	Data Input
1. Activity.	Reporting Command authorized funds,with Activity Address Code (AAC).
2. Appn.	FY appropriation authorized to procure items reported.
3. Subhead 6001 Command Support Equipment.	Include only items authorized under this subhead. Use separate report as directed for other programs such as: Physical Security Equipment(RCN 60032), Telephone Systems (RCN 60052), Garrison Mobile, or ADP equipment.
4. CMD Activity.	Indicate short command title of activity where equipment will be placed.
5. Ref No.	Indicate reference number from list of approved requirements. (This number is assigned only at Headquarters Marine Corps for budget submissions, emergency requirements, or reprioritized listings. The reference number must be included in all future correspondence related to the item.)
6a. Item Nomen.	Provide short descriptive name ofitem from original budget submission.
6b. Type.	Equipment Classification - BG, OE, GP, EN, FS, UE, CL4.
7. Budget.	(a) Quantity requested in original budget submit. (b) Cost is estimated unit price submitted in original budget.
8. Current Actual.	(a) Quantity actually procured. (b) Current total actual procurement cost.
9. Other/Under $15,000.	For HQMC use only.
10. FY Funds Authorized.	Fiscal year of funds authorized/used for procurement of this item.
11. FY Bud Requirement.	Indicate FY item was approved in budget.
12. Staff Action.	For HQMC use only.

Data Element No./Title.	Data Input
13. Staff Comments.	For HQMC use only.
14. New Prioritization.	Indicate prioritization No. in current FY prioritization request. (Use only consecutive numbers (no alphas) to indicate desired order of priority for procurement.) The command has the flexibility to revise the priority at any time for items not yet funded or in the procurement process.
15. Old Prioritization No.	Indicate Pri No. in original budget submission.
16. Status.	Indicate if item is (a) committed, with projected contract award date, (b) obligated date (c) received date or (d) completed date. Item status must be reported till completed (item expended and PA ID assigned).
17. Projected Obligated (Obl) Date.	Estimated date (month and year) to obligate funds dependent on cost receipt of applicable certification. Lead time should be revised whenever changes occur, to avoid withdrawal of funds for nonobligation.
18. Approved PD.	Indicate if procurement documentation (PD), (a) economic analysis, (b) equipment specifications, and (c) logistics support plan, is complete and requirement approved and validated for initiation of procurement action.
19. Remarks.	Provide mandatory data: (a) Certificate of Nonavailability (CNA) number and expiration date for class 4 items; (b) the assigned Plant Account ID number for receipted items must be reported to complete each item report. Other data such as: item canceled or procurement deferred, etc., should also be reported.
20. Funds Authorized.	Indicate total amount CMC authorized under this RCN for this FY as shown in on-hand documentation.
21. Funds Committed.	Indicate amount committed on requisitions but not obligated.
22. Funds Obligated.	Indicate amount actually obligated through signed contracts or acknowledge requisitions. Funds are not considered obligated unless reported in official accounting records.
23. Funds Expended.	Indicate amount of funds disbursed.
24. Funds Uncommitted.	Indicate amount of funds still available, pending submission of requisitions for procurement action or residual amounts excess from obligated and/or expended actions.

Input is required for all applicable data elements on a single list for each fiscal year and RCN. Submit the report on 8-1/2 in x 11 in paper. Submit the report quarterly to CMC (LFS) before the 10th day of January, April, July, and October for the preceding quarter. Computer output should be reduced to this size if necessary. Submission of computer data with the status report through a wide-area network (ELMS) or computer disks is recommended and encouraged.

GARRISON PROPERTY POLICY MANUAL
PERSONNEL SUPPORT EQUIPMENT (PSE)
ANNUAL INVENTORY REPORT
REPORT CONTROL SYMBOL DN-7110-03

ACTIVITY: ____________

DATE OF INVENTORY: _______ FY: ___________

POC: _________ AUTOVON NO.: ___________

	BEQ/BOQ	ADMIN. OFFICE	MESSHALL	TOTAL
A. INVENTORY VALUATION				
1. VALUE ($) OF PSE INVENTORY PRIOR YEAR	___	___	___	___
2. VALUE OF PSE ACQUIRED	___	___	___	___
a. New Acquisitions	___	___	___	___
b. Excess	___	___	___	___
c. Collateral Equipment for MILCON Projects	___	___	___	___
3. VALUE OF PSE DISPOSALS	___	___	___	___
4. VALUE ($) OF PSE INVENTORY CURRENT YEAR	___	___	___	___
5. TOTAL INVENTORY VALUATION: (Total Inventory Valuation (provide narrative if amount varies more than 10 percent from prior year)	___	___	___	___
B. BUDGET REQUIREMENTS				
1. BEQ/BOQ				
Sleeping (Bed, Secretary, Chair, Rug)	___			___
Living (Sofa, Chair, Table, Lamp)	___			___
Lounge (Seating, Game Tables)	___			___
Equipment Washer/Dryer, Vacuum, Refrigerator)	___			___
Total	___			___

PERSONNEL SUPPORT EQUIPMENT (PSE)
ANNUAL INVENTORY REPORT

	BEQ/BOQ	ADMIN. OFFICE	MESSHALL	TOTAL
2. ADMINISTRATIVE OFFICE				
Desk		___		___
Chair		___		___
Systems Work Stations		___		___
File Cabinets		___		___
Conference/Work Table		___		___
Bookcase		___		___
Credenza		___		___
Total		___		___
3. MESSHALL				
Tables			___	___
Chairs			___	___
Booths			___	___
Drapes			___	___
Decor			___	___
Total			___	___
4. SPECIAL PROJECT REQUIREMENTS				
(Type Project)	___	___	___	___
(Type Project)	___	___	___	___
Total	___	___	___	___
5. VALUE OF PSE REQUIREMENTS				
a. Prior Year Unfunded Deficiencies	___	___	___	___
b. Current Year New Requirements	___	___	___	___
c. New PSE Procurement Requirements	___	___	___	___
d. Value of On-Hand Reparable PSE	___	___	___	___
e. Total Requirements Budget	___	___	___	___

PERSONNEL SUPPORT EQUIPMENT (PSE)
ANNUAL INVENTORY REPORT

	EQ/BOQ	ADMIN. OFFICE	MESSHALL	TOTAL
C. FUNDS ALLOCATED, OBLIGATED, AND BUDGETED				
1. FUNDS OBLIGATED PRIOR FY				
CMC Allocated Funds				
Procurement	___	___	___	___
Repair	___	___	___	___
Command Financial Ceiling				
Procurement	___	___	___	___
Repair	___	___	___	___
Collateral Equipment for MILCON Projects	___	___	___	___
2. FUNDS OBLIGATED CURRENT FY				
CMC Allocated Funds				
Procurement	___	___	___	___
Repair	___	___	___	___
Command Financial Ceiling				
Procurement	___	___	___	___
Repair	___	___	___	___
Collateral Equipment for MILCON Projects	___	___	___	___
3. FUNDS BUDGETED FOR BY				
CMC Allocated Funds				
Procurement	___	___	___	___
Repair	___	___	___	___
Command Financial Ceiling				
Procurement	___	___	___	___
Repair	___	___	___	___
Collateral Equipment for MILCON Projects	___	___	___	___

PERSONNEL SUPPORT EQUIPMENT (PSE)
ANNUAL INVENTORY REPORT

	BEQ/BOQ	ADMIN. OFFICE	MESSHALL	TOTAL
4. FUNDS BUDGETED FOR BY + 1				
CMC Allocated Funds				
Procurement	___	___	___	___
Repair	___	___	___	___
Command Financial Ceiling				
Procurement	___	___	___	___
Repair	___	___	___	___
Collateral Equipment for MILCON Project	___	___	___	___
Total	___	___	___	___

Submit the PSE Annual Inventory Report to CMC (LFS) before 15 September.

GARRISON PROPERTY POLICY MANUAL
INSTRUCTIONS FOR:
PERSONNEL SUPPORT EQUIPMENT ANNUAL INVENTORY REPORT
REPORT CONTROL SYMBOL DN-7110-03

1. ACTIVITY. Enter the reporting command authorized funds.

2. DATE OF INVENTORY. Enter the date the inventory was started.

3. FISCAL YEAR. Enter the current fiscal year the budget is prepared.

4. POC. Enter the activity point of contact for the PSE program.

5. DSN NO. Enter the DSN telephone number for the POC.

6. INVENTORY VALUATION (A)

   a. VALUE ($) OF PSE INVENTORY PRIOR YEAR (A1). Enter the dollar value of the inventory reported the previous year. Provide the value for each facility category (BEQ/BOQ, administrative office or messhall) and the total value for the three categories.

   b. VALUE OF PSE ACQUIRED (A2)

      (1) NEW ACQUISITIONS (A2a). Enter the acquisition value of all PSE procured since the last inventory. Provide the value for each facility category and the total value for the three categories.

      (2) EXCESS (A2b). Enter the original acquisition cost, if available, or the fair market value of similar items, of all PSE acquired since the last inventory. Provide the value for each facility category and the total for the three categories.

      (3) COLLATERAL EQUIPMENT FOR MILCON PROJECTS (MCON CE) (A2c). Enter the acquisition cost of PSE procured as MCON CE For MILCON projects since the last inventory. Provide the value for each facility category and the total for the three categories.

   c. VALUE OF PSE DISPOSALS (A3). Enter the acquisition value of PSE sent to disposal or transferred to another activity since the last inventory. Provide the value for each facility category and the total value for the three categories.

   d. VALUE ($) OF PSE INVENTORY CURRENT YEAR (A4). Enter the PSE value generated from the current physical inventory. Provide the value for each facility category and the total value for the three categories.

   e. TOTAL INVENTORY VALUATION (A5). To compute the total value for each facility category take the value for the prior year inventory plus new acquisitions plus excess plus MCON CE minus disposals. Provide a narrative to explain if the difference between the current year PSE value and the total inventory valuation varies plus or minus 10 percent. Indicate if causative research and records reconciliation were performed.

7. BUDGET REQUIREMENTS (B)

a. BEQ/BOQ (B1); ADMINISTRATIVE OFFICE (B2); MESSHALL (B3). Enter the dollar value of actual requirements identified since the last inventory to repair, replace, or refurbish major PSE items used in each facility category (BEQ/BOQ, administrative offices or messhalls and any special requirements). Provide the requirements total for each category.

b. SPECIAL PROJECT REQUIREMENTS (B4). Enter project requirements for new PSE, but not covered under any other program described in this Manual. Briefly describe the project. Planned or authorized funds should not limit the budget requirements reported.

c. VALUE OF PSE REQUIREMENTS (B5)

(1) PRIOR YEAR UNFUNDED DEFICIENCIES (B5a). Enter deficiencies from prior year requirements not funded at the CMC or local level. Provide the value for each facility category and the total value for the three categories.

(2) CURRENT YEAR NEW REQUIREMENTS (B5b). Enter PSE requirements identified since the prior year inventory. Provide the value for each facility category and the total value for the three categories.

(3) NEW PSE REQUIREMENTS (B5c). Enter the requirements scheduled for replacement or augmentation through procurement.

(4) VALUE OF ON-HAND REPAIRABLE PSE (B5d). Enter the original value of usable and reparable PSE planned for maintenance or refurbishment. Provide the value for each facility category and the total value for the three categories.

(5) TOTAL REQUIREMENTS BUDGET (B5e). To compute the total add the requirements identified in B5a through B5d for each facility category and the total column.

8. FUNDS ALLOCATED, OBLIGATED, AND BUDGETED (C)

a. FUNDS OBLIGATED PRIOR FY (C1). Indicate the amount and source (CMC or local) of funds used in the prior year to procure replacement or MCON CE or to repair PSE (e.g., refurbish mattresses or refinish wood and metal furniture) for each facility category and the total column.

b. FUNDS OBLIGATED CURRENT FY (C2). Indicate the amount and source (CMC or local) of funds used in the current year to procure replacement or MCON CE or to repair PSE (e.g., refurbish mattresses or refinish wood and metal furniture) for each facility category and the total column. Funds allocated from CMC, available at the start of the fiscal year, should be obligated for known requirements early in the fiscal year.

c. FUNDS BUDGETED FOR BY (C3). Indicate the amount and source (CMC or local) of funds planned for use in the next budget year to procure replacement or MCON CE or to repair PSE (e.g., refurbish mattresses or refinish wood and metal furniture) for each facility category and the total column. This amount should reflect CMC estimates for PSE and MCON CE fund allocation and any local ceiling established for PSE used to reduce current PSE deficiencies.

c. <u>FUNDS BUDGETED FOR BY + 1 (C4)</u>. Indicate the amount and source (CMC or local) of funds planned for use in fiscal year after the next budget year to procure replacement or MCON CE or to repair PSE (e.g., refurbish mattresses or refinish wood and metal furniture) for each facility category and the total column. This amount should reflect CMC budget estimates for PSE and MCON CE funds and the projected ceiling PSE used to reduce PSE deficiencies and projected requirements.

Submit the PSE report annually to CMC (LFS) before 15 September. Message format is acceptable.

(RCS EXEMPT)

MINOR PROPERTY REQUIREMENTS

ACTIVITY:
FY:
POC:

DATE PREPARED:
APPN/SH:
AUTOVON NO.:

A. DEFICIENCIES OVER CORE

	ITEM NOMEN	NEW	(N)	CY REPLACE	CY OTY	BY COST	BY OTY	BY+1 COST	BY+1 OTY	BY+2 COST	BY+2 OTY
1. ACQUISITION											
$300 - $5,000											
$5,000 - $15,000											
2. MAINTENANCE											
$300 - $5,000											
Over $5,000											
TOTAL (1+2)											

B. TOTAL REQUIREMENTS ESTIMATES

	ITEM NOMEN	NEW	(N)	CY REPLACE	CY OTY	BY COST	BY OTY	BY+1 COST	BY+1 OTY	BY+2 COST	BY+2 OTY
1. ACQUISITION											
$300 - $5,000											
$5,000 - $15,000											
2. MAINTENANCE											
$300 - $5,000											
Over $5,000											
TOTAL (1+2)											

MINOR PROPERTY REQUIREMENTS (cont'd.)

C. ALLOCATIONS, OBLIGATIONS, ESTIMATIONS

	$300 - $5,000	$5,000 - $15,000
1. TOTAL FUNDS ALLOCATED THE PAST YEAR		
a. Acquisition		
HQMC Managed Program	________	________
Local Funds	________	________
b. Repair Costs		
HQMC Managed Program	________	________
Local Funds	________	________
TOTAL (a + b)	________	________
2. TOTAL OBLIGATIONS FOR THE PAST YEAR		
a. Acquisition		
HQMC Managed Program	________	________
Local Funds	________	________
b. Repair Costs		
HQMC Managed Program	________	________
Local Funds	________	________

MINOR PROPERTY REQUIREMENTS (cont'd.)

	$300 - $5,000	$5,000 - $15,000
c. Dollar Value acquired through excess		
Disposals	__________	__________
Transfers	__________	__________
d. Dollar Value of		
Disposals	__________	__________
Transfers	__________	__________
TOTAL (a+b+c+d)	__________	__________
3. ESTIMATES FOR BUDGET YEAR		
a. Acquisition	__________	__________
b. Repair Costs	__________	__________
TOTAL (a+b)	__________	__________

INSTRUCTIONS FOR:
MINOR PROPERTY REQUIREMENTS

1. ACTIVITY. Enter the reporting command authorized funds.

2. DATE PREPARED. Enter the date the inventory was started.

3. FISCAL YEAR. Enter the current fiscal year the budget is prepared.

4. APPN/SH. Enter the appropriation and subhead for funds used to procure, repair, or maintain minor property.

5. POC. Enter the activity point of contact for the Minor Property program.

6. DSN NO. Enter the DSN telephone number for the POC.

7. DEFICIENCIES OVER CORE

   a. ACQUISITION. Identify minor property procurement requirements over the core funding level for the activity. Provide the aggregate total cost for item groups with a unit cost between $300 to $5,000 and $5,000 to 15,000 such as maintenance or shop tools, office equipment or laborsaving devices. Beside the group nomenclature, identify as new or replacement items. Provide the total required for the current fiscal year and the next 3 budget years.

   b. MAINTENANCE. Identify requirements for garrison (plant and minor) property maintenance, over the core funding level, to include in-house or contract repairs for each cost category. Repair will include requirement costs for property from $300 to $5,000 and over $5,000

8. TOTAL REQUIREMENTS ESTIMATE. Identify the sum for the activity of the core and deficiency (described in paragraph 7 above) requirements for minor property for acquisition and for maintenance.

9. TOTAL FUNDS ALLOCATED THE PAST YEAR

   a. Enter the funds allocated for minor property acquisition or repair during the previous year. Indicate funds provided directly from HQMC or through local funding authority for each cost category.

   b. Include funds for property repair or maintenance with a cost from $300 to $5,000 and over $5,000.

   c. To compute the total add the obligations for acquisition and repair.

10. TOTAL OBLIGATIONS FOR THE PAST YEAR

   a. Enter the funds obligated for minor property acquisition or repair during the previous year. Indicate funds provided directly from HQMC or through local funding authority for each cost category. Repair will include funds for property with a unit cost from $300 to $5,000 and over $5,000.

   b. Indicate the acquisition value of minor property transferred from another activity or service or acquired as excess from a DRMO.

c. Indicate the acquisition valve of minor property sent to the DRMO or to another activity or service during the previous year.

d. To compute the total add to the obligations for acquisition, the repair costs and the value of acquired excess minus the value of disposals or transfers.

11. <u>ESTIMATES FOR BUDGET YEAR</u>. Indicate the estimated funds planned for acquisition and repair from all sources for the next budget year. Compute the total.

TABLE 1: SAMPLE ECONOMICS ANALYSIS

ACTIVITY: __________ DATE PREPARED: __________

A. PROJECT COSTS: Alternative A ITEM: Reprographic Equipment

PROJECT YEAR	NONRECURRING INVENTSMENT COST	RECURRING OPERATIONS	ANNUAL COST	DISCOUNT FACTOR	DISCOUNT ANNUAL COST
1.	$90,000	$12,000	$102,000	1.000	$102,000
2.		$12,000	$ 12,000	0.954	$ 11,448
3.		$12,000	$ 12,000	0.867	$ 10,404
4.		$12,000	$ 12,000	0.788	$ 9,456
5.		$12,000	$ 12,000	0.717	$ 8,604
6.		$12,000	$ 12,000	0.652	$ 7,824
7.		$12,000	$ 12,000	0.592	$ 7,104
8.		$12,000	$ 12,000	0.538	$ 6,456
9.		$12,000	$ 12,000	0.489	$ 5,868
10.		$12,000	$ 12,000	0.445	$ 5,340
TOTALS	$90,000	$120,000	$210,000	7.042	$174,504

TOTALS PROJECT COST (DISCOUNTED)	$174,504
UNIFORM ANNUAL COST (WITHOUT TERMINAL VALUE)	$ 21,000
LESS TERMINAL VALUE (DISCOUNTED - $5,000 X .455	$ 2,225
NET TOTAL PROJECT COST	$172,279
UNIFORM ANNUAL COST (WITH TERMINAL VALUE)	$ 17,228

B. SOURCE/DERIVATION OF COST ESTIMATES (Narrative):

1. NONRECURRING COSTS: (GSA Schedule/Vendor Estimate)

2. RECURRING COSTS: (Maintenance/Operations/Training) EXPECTED

C. BENEFITS (Narrative):

1. Tangible Benefits

2. Intangible Benefits

D. COST AVOIDANCE:

TABLE 2: COST COMPARISON FORM

L-34

INSTRUCTIONS FOR: ECONOMIC ANALYSIS

The Economic Analysis consists of two parts, project costs and cost comparison. The present value analysis includes project costs, benefits, and cost avoidance sections. Projects costs are computed for each procurement, lease, status quo, or other alternative. The cost comparison compares costs for each alternative for the life of the project on an annual and total cost and discount basis. MCO 7000.12 provides additional guidance to perform an economic analysis for ongoing and proposed Marine Corps programs, projects, and activities.

Table 1

1. Activity. Provide information to identify the activity and functional user.

2. Date Prepared. Indicate date analysis completed or updated.

3. Project Costs. Competitive procurement requires comparison of several alternatives, the baseline or current status, lease, and procurement options.

   a. Nonrecurring Costs. For each alternative, identify the nonrecurring equipment start up or initial one-time costs.

   b. Recurring Costs. Identify estimated O&M costs for the life of the equipment.

   c. Annual Cost. Compute the total actual cost for each estimated year the equipment will be used.

   d. Discount. Use the 10 percent discount factors for 10 years as shown in the format. The number of years may be reduced to coincide with the equipment life expectancy.

   e. Discounted Annual Cost. Add the nonrecurring and recurring costs and multiply the sum by the discount factor. Total for each year and total each column.

   f. Total Project Cost (Discounted). Enter the total of the total discounted annual cost column.

   g. Uniform Annual Cost (Discounted). Divide the total project cost by the number of project years.

   h. Less Terminal Value (Discounted). Determine the salvage value, turn-in value, or terminal cost. Compute the discount value based on the terminal year of the project. (For example, the present value of the $5,000 salvage value is $2,225 after 10 years).

   i. Net Total Project Cost. Subtract the discounted terminal value from the discounted total project cost.

4. Source/Derivation of Cost Estimates. Indicate the source of price and item data used to estimate the project costs. Use GSA or vendor schedules as a basis for nonrecurring competitive procurement. Use historical data or manufacturer estimates to develop recurring costs.

5. Benefits

   a. Tangible Benefits. Identify known or projected tangible benefits such as reduced personnel costs operationing hours, and maintenance costs.

   b. Intangible Benefits. Identify known or expected intangible benefits such as increased productivity, improved accuracy, and reduced transportation time.

6. Cost Avoidance. Identify any costs avoided with this procurement such as avoid fines, avoid hiring additional personnel, or eliminate short-term equipment repair costs.

Table 2

1. Item. Identify equipment nomenclature.

2. Cost Comparison. Compare the costs of each alternative for the average equipment life. Compare the baseline or status with one or two procurement options and a lease option, if applicable. The cost elements should include all costs attributable to the equipment acquisition and operation. Compute the subtotal by adding all cost elements in the column for each alternative.

3. Personnel Costs. Compare personnel costs if there is a difference. If the costs are the same for all options, do not compare these costs.

4. Total Costs. Compute the total costs for each alternative and multiply by the discount factor for life cycle year. Use the discount factors from Table 1 above.

5. Differences. Compute the difference between the total costs for each option or between the options and the baseline, if used.

6. Cumulative Differences. Compute the cumulative differences for all years compared to identify the least cost option.

7. Annual Cost. Cost the total cost before a discount factor is applied.

PLACEHOLDER FOR DOD PROPERTY RECORD

DOD PROPERTY RECORD

SECTION I - INVENTORY RECORD

ELECTRICAL CHARACTERISTICS

SECTION II - INSPECTION RECORD

SAMPLE

INSTRUCTIONS FOR:
DOD PROPERTY RECORD

A. PLANT PROPERTY. The DoD Property Record should be prepared following guidance in NavCompt Manual, volume 3, paragraph 036205. Specific attention should be given to the following blocks:

1. Block 3: ID/Government Tag No. The PA number is the unique ID number assigned to each item of plant property. For garrison mobile equipment, the tag number will include "USMCGM" plus the HQMC assigned registration number as described in paragraph 8003.3 of the manual.

2. Block 4: Commodity Code. The standard commodity code (SCC) or plant equipment codes (PEC) used to report class 3 plant property are contained in the DLA cataloging handbooks entitled "Federal Supply Classification (FSC)" available on microfiche. PEC's are contained in Marine Corps directives in the 4870 series of the IPE handbook. The PEC is a 12-digit subclassification system within the framework of the FSC system to encode primary characteristics of items of IPE, class 4 property.

3. Block 5: Stock Number. National stock numbers (NSN) should be used to identify the item or the 4-digit FSC assigned to that type of equipment. Local stock numbers should not be used.

4. Block 7: Type Code. The type codes for plant property are contained in NavCompt Manual, volume 3, paragraph 036206.6.

5. Block 15: Manufacturers' Codes (MFC). MFC's are contained in the DLA cataloging handbooks, entitled "Federal Supply Code for Manufacturers, United States and Canada."

6. Blocks 18-21: Dimensions. Obtain the equipment dimensions following the guidance in NavCompt Manual, volume 3, paragraph 036205.

7. Block 22: Certificate of Non-Availability. Guidance is provided in paragraph 7003.4 of this Manual and in the NavCompt Manual, volume 3, paragraph 036205.

8. Block 25: Contract Number. Enter the complete contract number used to procure the item.

9. Block 26: Description. Enter the complete item description using DLA Catalog H2-3, as applicable.

10. Block 28: Location. Enter the command location and the user location and custodian.

11. Block 29: Possessor Code. Enter the activity accounting number (AAN) of the activity in possession of the equipment. This is not the UIC of the unit. The AAN can be found in the NavCompt Manual, volume 2.

12. Block 52: Condition Code. Enter the 2-digit supply disposal code found in appendix G and the NavCompt Manual, volume 3, paragraph 036206.5.

13. Block 54: Remarks. Enter the requisition number and appropriation data used to acquire the equipment.

B. MINOR PROPERTY. The database for minor property will include the following:

1. Identification (ID) Number. Enter the unique ID number assigned to each item from the block of ID numbers contained in appendix I.

2. Item Nomenclature. Enter the noun name and descriptive data. For example, record a chair as chair, rotary, executive, class A, with arms; or chair, desk, straight, without arms.

3. Model Number, Serial Number, Manufacturer. Enter the manufacturers' model and/or serial number attached to the item and the manufacturers' code number (MFC).

4. Quantity or Item Count. When several items are included on a single record, indicate the total number of the same model and nomenclature. The individual ID numbers for each item will be included in the property record.

5. Location and Custodian. Enter the physical location and name or code used to identify the custodian for the item.

6. Acquisition Date. Enter the contract obligation date.

7. Acquisition Cost. Enter the actual cost to acquire the property. In the case of donations, use the fair market value.

8. Date of Last Inventory. Enter the month, day, and year when last inventory was completed for the item.

9. Requisition Number and Purchase Number. Enter the requisition number and the purchase number.

Record Field	Legend	DD 1342 Field	Additional Guidelines
1	Class (TYPE)	N/A	Review items for assignment to the correct property class, 3 or 4. Industrial Plant Equipment (IPE). Information related to class 4 plant property is in Marine Corps directives in the 4870 series of IPE handbooks. Use MCO P4870.60, enclosure (1), for additional guidance. Report all controlled items (Program Code CI) authorized for use in MCO P4400.82 which meet the plant property criteria as class 3 property. IPE-type items issued as controlled items do not meet criteria for class 4 property and are not reported to DIPEC.
2-13	Standard Commodity Code or Plant Equipment Code (PROD EQUIP)	4	Identify items with the proper SCC/PEC, as appropriate. SCC's are in the following Defense Logistics Agency (DLA) cataloging handbooks entitled "Federal Supply Classification": a. H2-1 Part 1, Groups and Classes. b. H2-2. Part 2, Numeric Index of Classes. c. H2-3. Part 3, Alphabetic Index. PEC's are a 12-digit subclassification system within the Federal Supply Classification (FSC) system framework to encode primary characteristics of IPE items. The PEC's are in Marine Corps directives in the 4870 series of IPE handbooks. Use National Stock Numbers (NSN), if available, to identify the item. Otherwise, the 4-digit FSC is sufficient. When using the NSN, omit the first digit of the national code (e.g., 7430-0-123-4567).
14-25	Plant Account Number (PLANT ACCOUNT)	3	Enter the 12-digit identification number assigned to the item as delinated in chapter 8 of this Manual. To report Garrison Mobile Equipment (including vehicles, materials handling equipment, and construction/engineer equipment), indicate the

Record Field	Legend	DD 1342 Field	Additional Guidelines
			assigned registration number in lieu of the plant account number. (For vehicles, use "USMCGM" in lieu of the Unit identification Code in block 3 of DD-1342.) The CMC (LFS) controls the assignment of plant account numbers.
26-30	Activity Accounting (AAN)	13	Enter appropriate UIC of fiscal office with plant property accountability (PAA) for activity in possession of item.
31-37	Blank (ACT-CODE)	N/A	Reserved for local use, see paragraph 6 of the general guidance.
38-39	Year Manufactured (MFG YR)	8	Use the last two digits of year manufactured. Do not use N/A.
40	Estimated Year Manufactured (EST MFG YR)	8	Enter the letter "E" if year manufactured is estimated. If not estimated, leave blank.
41-44	Month and Year Installed (INST DATE)	N/A	Use two digits for the month and last two digits of the year installed. Do not use N/A.
45-46	Condition Code (CON)	52	Update the 2-digit condition code before submission of each report, when applicable. The supply and disposal codes are in appendix G. Once equipment is placed in use, the code is A4.
47-48	Estimated Replacement Year (REPL YEAR)	N/A	Guidelines to determine life expectancy and estimated replacement year for selected in-use items are in appendix J and the NavCompt Manual. Compute from the date the DD-1342 is prepared. Budget requirements for the out-years are based on reported REPL YEAR. The importance of this field can not be overemphasized. Revise this field if inspection indicated the useful life will be reduced or extended.

Record Field	Legend	DD 1342 Field	Additional Guidelines
			a. The entry for fiscal year 2000 is "00." b. If the item will not be replaced, enter "NA". No other letter abbreviation should be used in the field. The RPL YR shall reflect the fiscal year (FY) the item will most probably be budgeted for replacement (FY 1994, 1995 and out-years.)
49-55	Acquisition Cost (ACQ COST)	6	Enter the unit cost rounded to whole dollars omitting dollar signs and commas. If cost is estimated, cite the comparable current replacement cost. The cost shall include standard accessories procured and delivered with the basic unit. The cost should also include transportation and initial set-up charges. Enter the total costs for each SCC/PEC and for each property class.
56	Cost Data (CD)	N/A	Enter "I" for Investment or "E" for Expense items. All items classified as plant property, regardless of where used, shall be shown as expense (E) if procured with O&MMC funds and as investment (I) if procured with PMC funds.
57-70	Description of Item (DESCRIPTION)	N/A	Review all item descriptions. Use descriptive nouns in DLA Catalog H2-3, as applicable. Do not use commercial trade names unless absolutely necessary. Use Marine Corps equipment codes (MEC) to report Garrison Mobile Equipment (including vehicles, materials handling equipment and construction/engineer equipment) or portions of the abbreviated nomenclature used in MCO P11240.106. For example, "1201 TRK DUMP," "1801 FORKLIFT," "3702 SWEEPMAG" (magnet sweeper). Use all spaces necessary to identify the item with actual descriptive noun first, followed with the most appropriate words to describe the item. Only understandable abbreviations are acceptable. Nouns which describe more than one type item are not acceptable. For example: Not Acceptable Acceptable TABLE TABLE, BAND SAW

Record Field	Legend	DD 1342 Field	Additional Guidelines	
			<u>Not Acceptable</u>	<u>Acceptable</u>
			GEN	3314 GEN 100KW (Mobile)
			GEN	GEN 300 KW STAT (Stationary)
			RADIO	RADIO AN/PRC-47 (Tactical)
			AN/TGC	TT AN/TGC-6
			FIXTURE	
			DEVICE	
			2540-1	
			STRONG BACK	
			BATH	
			BAR	
71-75	Manufacturers' Code (MFG CODE)	15	Use the manufacturers' codes in the DLA cataloging handbooks: a. H4/8, Commercial and Government Entity Code (CAGE), Sections A & B b. H4/8, NATO Supply Code for Manufacturers Sections C & D	
76-77	Program Code (PROG CODE)	N/A	Identify the property code of the separate program used to procure the plant account item. Use only the following codes: a. <u>CI</u>. Report tactical equipment used only in garrison as directed in MCO P4400.82. b. <u>CM</u>. Items used in Clubs. c. <u>CO</u>. Items used in commissaries. d. <u>DP</u>. Automated data processing equipment. e. <u>EN</u>. Environmental protection equipment. f. <u>FS</u>. Food service equipment for messhalls. g. <u>GM</u>. Garrison Mobile Equipment, includes vehicles material handling	

Record Field	Legend	DD 1342 Field	Additional Guidelines

equipment, construction/engineer equipment, and mobile-type generators.

h. PE. Personal capital plant equipment used to provide operating support to the commands.

i. PH. Authorized photographic equipment.

j. PS. Physical security equipment.

k. SS. Special services equipment acquired with appropriated funds or MWR equipment accounted for as plant property.

l. TR. Authorized training equipment.

m. WH. Warehouse storage equipment Includes shelving and retrieval systems.

Note the following distinctions:

a. Use the code GM for GME and the code PE for personal capital plant equipment (PE). Use the assigned GM registration number in lieu of a plant account number to eliminate confusion between GM and PE budget programs.

b. Code personal capital equipment used in photograph or training departments as PE, not photographic (PH). For example, code copiers used in the photographic department as PE.

c. Code special services equipment accounted for as plant property, such as "GYM SET" or "Bath Sauna" as special services (SS) equipment.

d. Similar items may have more than one functional use. For example, code a floor scrubber, whether used in multiple locations or solely in a messhall as PE. Code a dishwasher as FS if used in the messhall or SS if used in the club.

e. Report controlled items defined as class

Record Field	Legend	DD 1342 Field	Additional Guidelines
			Manual as CI. CMC budgets, procures, and issues tactical material reported as controlled items to field activities through established allowances.
78-80	BLANK	N/A	Reserved for local use. See paragraph 6 of the general guidance.

GARRISON PROPERTY POLICY MANUAL
PLANT PROPERTY REPORT
GENERAL GUIDANCE (RCS DN-7321-01)

1. OSD imposed a requirement to furnish, for budgetary purposes, a report of personal capital plant equipment requirements for 6 out-years. The format eliminates unnecessary data and incorporates essential information required for HQMC use. The plant account report with projected replacement items will substantiate the out-years requirements budget. Review the report to report new equipment within the time frames specified. (NavCompt Manual, paragraph, 036202).

2. Submit the semiannual inventory report of classes 3 and 4 plant property in the mechanized report format to CMC (FDL) before 15 April and 15 October (see paragraph 8011) using the automated Marine Corps Data Network (MCDN) data transmission capabilities. The format is mandatory for all data to ensure compatibility for further information analysis, processing and reproduction. Use the following data set name for MCDN submission:

```
XXXXX.PLNTPROP.I7503P14.CLASS34X(+1)
DCB=(XXXXX,MDSCB,RECFM=FB,LRECL=80,BLKSIZE=6400,
UNIT=SYSDA)
(XXXXX will contain appropriate first level
qualifier.)
```

The changes above are:

a. "X" in CLASS34X will only be used when two or more activities are transmitting through the same CDPA/RACS with the same first qualifier in the DSN. Senior activity will add the letter A, nest junior activity B and so forth to the last qualifier of the DSN (For example, CLASS#$A, CLASS#$V, etc) depending on how many other activities are utilizing the same first qualifier in the DSN.

b. The (+1) is to facilitate retransmission of data.

c. XXXXX, MDSCB is a must for creation of Generational Data Sets.

3. Report separate totals for class 3 expense and investment categories with a grand total of all class 3 property.

4. Report the total cost of class 4 investment plant property.

5. The total costs reported in each property class should substantiate the costs reflected on the Reconciliation of Plant Account Report (NavCompt Form 167) for the corresponding period. Any significant differences should be reconciled prior to submission of the reports.

6. Space is provided in the report format for use of local data elements. The data in this space will permit the activity to maintain control of property in their custody.

7. Commands with accounting responsibility for more than one activity shall submit reports for each activity. Marine Corps activities with Navy and Marine Corps accounting shall submit the report for all property regardless of funding source on a single Marine Corps report to CMC (FDL).

8. The information in the inventory reports must be accurate to fulfill higher authority requirements.

9. Plant property with a unit cost equal to or greater than $5,000 shall be accounted for as plant property. Property valued at less than $5,000 shall be accounted for a minor property per the acquisition criteria and accountability rules contained in the NavCompt Manual, paragraph 036700.

APPENDIX M

ACTIVITIES REQUIRED TO SUBMIT PLANT PROPERTY REPORTS

Command	Unit Identifier Code	Data Processing Installation Code
1st MCD	67011	1861
12th MCD	67019	1866
4th MCD	67013	1862
4th MarDiv	68479	1833
4th MAW	67021	1836
6th MCD	67015	1863
8th MCD	67016	1864
MB 8th & I	67029	1869
9th MCD	67017	1865
Albany	67004	1834
Barstow	62204	1839
Beaufort	60169	1848
Camp Butler	67400	1802
Camp Elmore	67391	1816
Cherry Point	00146	1847
Camp Lejeune	67001	1853
Camp Pendleton	00681	1830
Camp Smith	67385	1800
El Toro	60050	1841
FMFLant Norfolk	67026	1815
HqBn Hend Hall	67353	1868
HQMC	00027	1867
Iwakuni	62613	1804
Kaneohe Bay	00318	1801
MCRSC	68522	1860
MCSA, KC	67443	1859
New River	62573	1849
Parris Island	00263	1828
Quantico	00264	1825
San Diego	00243	1837
Twentynine Palms	67399	1838
Tustin	62435	1844
Yuma	62974	1845

FMF UNITS REQUIRED TO REPORT ADPE

Command	Unit Identifier Code	Data Processing Installation Code
HQ FMFPac	67024	1803
1st MAW	57079	1805
3d FSSG	67436	1806
3d MarDiv	67360	1807
1st MarDiv	67448	1808
1st MarBde	67339	1809

Command	Unit Identifier Code	Data Processing Installation Code
3d MAW	55081	1810
7th MEB	55356	1811
1st MEF	55205	1812
3d MEF	55211	1813
1st FSSG	67446	1814
MB ADAK, AK	67285	1872
MB Subic Bay Luzon, Philippines	67033	9801
MB Guam	62293	9802
MB Hawaii	0348A	9803
MB Yokosuka, JA	62217	9804
HQ FMFLant	67026	1817
4th MEB	55209	1818
2d MAW	57080	1820
H&S Bn	55359	1822
2d MEF	55207	1824
2d MAW	57080	1846
2d FSSG	68408	1821
2d MarDiv	08321	1819
6th MEB	55208	1823
LFTCLant	67355	9805
LFTCPac	67271	9806

GARRISON PROPERTY POLICY MANUAL

INDEX

Paragraph

- G -

- H -

- I -

- P -

DEFENSE LOGISTICS AGENCY
HEADQUARTERS
CAMERON STATION
ALEXANDRIA, VIRGINIA 22304-6100

DLAR 4145.25
AR-700-68
NAVSUPINST 4440.128C
MCO 10330.2C
AFR 67-12

DLA-OW

16 Jan 90

DLA REGULATION
NO. 4145.25

STORAGE AND HANDLING OF COMPRESSED GASES AND LIQUIDS IN CYLINDERS, AND OF CYLINDERS

I. PURPOSE AND SCOPE. To prescribe policy, procedures, and responsibilities for the storage, handling, and quality surveillance of industrial and medical compressed gases (nonliquefied and liquefied) and the cylinders in which they are contained to assure optimum use of both the gases and the cylinders by all Department of Defense (DoD) and Defense Logistics Agency (DLA) activities. Aerosol-type containers currently in the military supply system are not considered in this regulation. When transporting aerosol containers refer to Title 49 Code of Federal Regulations (CFR). Flammable aerosols should be stored as Class 1A flammable liquids as stated in NFPA 30, Flammable and Combustible Liquids Code. This regulation is applicable to HQ DLA and to all Defense Depots and Military Service storage activities that receive, store, issue, maintain, and perform associated services on compressed gases and gas cylinders managed by the Defense General Supply Center (DGSC) and the Defense Personnel Support Center (DPSC). This regulation has been coordinated with, and approved by, the Army, Navy, Air Force, and Marine Corps.

II. POLICY. It is policy that all compressed gases and gas cylinders in the DoD distribution system be classified uniformly as to condition status, that storage practices maintain serviceability with minimum costs, and that products delivered to customers are satisfactory for their intended use in all respects.

III. BACKGROUND

A. The compressed gases used by DLA and DoD activities are manufactured by both commercial production plants and military field activities. The manufacturing and quality requirements for each gas product are provided in Military, Federal, and commercial specifications. All DLA and DoD activities located in the continental United States (CONUS) are required to purchase their gas products from commercial sources that have negotiated supply contracts through the General Services Administration (GSA). Each contractor is to provide the desired gas product and the necessary services to retest and recondition the applicable cylinders to ensure they remain in safe and serviceable condition. Each using activity's requirements are provided to the GSA and a contract is negotiated annually. Overseas military requirements are satisfied by shipment of the desired products from CONUS, by local manufacture of the product onsite by the military activity, or by purchasing the desired products from host country commercial suppliers.

B. Verification of the quality of the purchased or manufactured product is conducted at the site of manufacture or at the product distributor's warehouse. Necessary testing is performed by the supplier's personnel under the surveillance of a Government representative, or records of the examination and tests are maintained by the supplier and made available to the Government upon request. Inspection and/or supplier verification testing is conducted under the surveillance of a Government Quality Assurance Representative (QAR). The quality of the gas product contained under pressure in a compressed gas cylinder will not change under normal storage and handling conditions; however, the condition of the cylinder may deteriorate and render the cylinder unsafe for further use. Procedures for the prevention and/or detection of these conditions are provided and defined in this regulation.

C. Gas cylinders purchased for the storage and shipment of compressed gas products for DLA and DoD activities are procured in accordance with Military and/or Federal specifications. These spec-

This DLAR supersedes DLAR 4145.25/AR-700-68/NAVSUPINST 4440.128B/MCO 10330.2B/AFR 67-12, 2 Sep 71.

ifications supplement United States Department of Transportation (DOT) manufacturing requirements with the necessary military design and marking requirements. The basic cylinder is manufactured to the desired DOT specification (e.g., 3AA, 4BA, 8A), then assembled into a complete cylinder with the desired valve, color code, and product identification designating its specific use. The fabrication of the cylinder by the manufacturer and the initial hydrostatic testing and recording of data by an independent inspection agency are under the surveillance of a Government QAR. Cylinders may be purchased and sent directly to a compressed gas filling installation for immediate use, or they may be shipped directly to a stock or depot storage facility where they may remain for an undetermined length of time. During any storage period, whether the cylinder is full or empty, its condition may deteriorate, causing it to become unsafe for further use. All persons who handle, use, and fill cylinders must be able to recognize deteriorating conditions and initiate action to have the cylinders reconditioned or removed from service. Any person offering a compressed gas for shipment must assure that the cylinder it is shipped in meets all design and manufacturing requirements of the applicable Federal, Military, and DOT specifications and that it has been retested and reconditioned in accordance with MIL-STD-1411, Inspection and Maintenance of Compressed Gas Cylinders, and DOT Title 49 CFR, Transportation. These documents and procedures are discussed in detail in enclosure 1 of this regulation.

D. Certain safety precautions must be exercised in the storage, handling, and use of compressed gases and of the cylinders in which they are contained. The primary precautions for compressed gases used by DoD activities are provided in enclosure 1 of this regulation. In addition to written precautions, the DoD has established a color coding system that identifies the primary and secondary safety hazards presented by each compressed gas or mixture of compressed gases. This system is outlined in MIL-STD-101B, Color Codes for Pipelines and Compressed Gas Cylinders. The system enables the gas user or cylinder handler to immediately identify the type of gas and the hazardous nature of the material contained in each cylinder (e.g., flammable, nonflammable, corrosive, poisonous, oxidizing). Additional information and further guidance may be obtained from the preparing and coordinating activities of this regulation, the local safety office or fire department, the manufacturer of the specific compressed gas, the Compressed Gas Association, the Hazardous Materials Technical Center (HMTC), or the DOT.

E. Cleaning, internal and external, is performed by the commercial supplier and/or vendor at the time of filling. Should cleaning become necessary during storage, materials used to clean the cylinders must be compatible with the gas or liquid to be put into the cylinders, or the gas or liquid previously in the empty cylinders. For instance, 1,1, trichloroethylene can explode.

IV. SIGNIFICANT CHANGES. This regulation has been completely revised and should be reviewed in its entirety.

V. RESPONSIBILITIES

A. The Chief, Depot Operations Division, Directorate of Supply Operations, HQ DLA (DLA-OW) will be responsible for monitoring and staff supervision of the DLA program for storage, handling, and use of compressed gases (nonliquefied and liquefied) in cylinders and for the overseas hydrostatic testing and reconditioning of cylinders.

B. Field Activities

1. The Commanders of DGSC and DPSC will:

a. Ensure the quality of compressed gases and gas cylinders that are procured or managed.

b. Provide guidance as needed to all DLA and DoD activities that store, handle, or use compressed gases to maintain an adequate and constant safety and quality control program.

c. Review the quality control and related technical aspects of this regulation annually and, in collaboration with DLA-OW, maintain appropriate constituent parts current.

2. The Commanders of DLA and DoD Storage and Using Activities that Furnish Special Support to DLA will:

a. Implement the requirements of this regulation.

b. Ensure that all persons who use, handle, maintain, and/or store compressed gases (nonliquefied and liquefied) contained in cylinders are aware of and comply with the provisions of this joint regulation and its enclosures.

c. Conduct inspections as required herein, and maintain concise records of such inspections.

d. Assign condition codes, and report in accordance with this regulation.

e. Maintain and segregate all full and empty serviceable, Supply Condition Code A cylinders in a safe and usable condition and ensure that all cylinders coded other than Supply Condition Code A are handled properly according to their condition.

f. Assure the use of Government-owned cylinders for the purchase of all compressed gases when a suitable cylinder can be identified.

g. Develop and maintain an accountability system for all commercially-owned cylinders used to supply compressed gases from local distributors using owner symbols and serial numbers.

h. Identify and return all non-Government-owned cylinders to their rightful owners, and ensure they are not returned to Defense Depot or DoD storage activity or reported to a DLA Supply Center as excess personal property. Assistance in identifying the commercial ownership symbols found on the shoulders of commercially-owned cylinders will be provided by the Defense General Supply Center, DGSC-ST, upon request. All non-Government-owned cylinders shall be processed by the holder as lost, abandoned, or unclaimed privately-owned personal property in accordance with DoD 4160.21-M, Defense Utilization and Disposal Manual, and section 8 of enclosure 1 of this regulation.

3. The Commander, Defense Reutilization and Marketing Service (DRMS) will:

a. Receive serviceable, condemned, and unserviceable gas cylinders from authorized activities in accordance with DoD 4160.21-M, and section 8 of enclosure 1 of this regulation.

b. Maintain all serviceable cylinders Supply Condition Code A in a safe and usable condition.

c. Dispose of serviceable, condemned, and unserviceable gas cylinders in accordance with DoD 4160.21-M.

d. Ensure that all Defense Reutilization and Marketing Service (DRMS) personnel who use, handle, maintain, and/or store gas cylinders are aware of and comply with the provisions of this joint regulation and its enclosures.

4. The Commanders of Department of Defense (DoD) Using Activities will:

a. Ensure that all personnel who use, handle, maintain, and/or store compressed gases or liquids contained in cylinders and gas cylinders are aware of and comply with the provisions of this joint regulation.

b. Maintain all Condition Code A compressed gas cylinders in a safe and usable condition and ensure that all compressed gas cylinders coded other than Condition Code A are handled properly according to their condition.

c. Report by the correct National Stock Number (NSN) and the correct Condition Code excess Government-owned industrial gas and liquid cylinders to DGSC and excess Government-owned medical gas and liquid cylinders to DPSC for disposition instructions.

d. Identify and return all contractor-owned, leased, or loaned cylinders to their rightful owners and ensure they are not reported to a DLA Center as excess. When a cylinder cannot be identified to a valid NSN or its ownership cannot be determined, disposition instructions shall be requested from the appropriate managing activity.

VI. PROCEDURES

A. The compressed gas cylinder is a unique item in the DLA supply system. Policies and procedures that apply to cylinders differ somewhat from those that govern other commodities. In addition to the many physical characteristics that are peculiar to cylinders and their contents, the regulations and procedures for storage, handling, transportation, and use of cylinders and their contents are published by industry and Government agencies outside the DoD.

B. Personnel who handle compressed gas cylinders must be familiar with the characteristics and hazards associated with compressed gases and liquids in cylinders, and with the statutes and regulations that control the inspection, storage, transportation, environmental impact, and disposal of cylinders and their contents. Adherence to the procedures and precautions as set forth in this regulation will ensure compliance with the requirements of Government and industry regulations and standards.

C. Detailed procedures are outlined in enclosures 1 and 2. Condition Codes as prescribed in the enclosures defined in DoD 4000.25-2-M, Military Standard Transaction Reporting and Accounting (MILSTRAP). Detailed inspection, maintenance, and reconditioning procedures to be incorporated in all cylinder filling and reconditioning contracts are contained in MIL-STD-1411. Additional storage, handling, and inspection procedures for cylinders used by the Air Force are contained in Air Force Technical Order TO-42B5-1-2.

D. Use of "Shall," "Must," and "Should." Certain words are used in this regulation to distinguish between practices that are mandatory and practices that are suggested to save time and effort. The words "shall" and "must" indicate actions that are mandatory and do not permit personnel to use their own judgment. "Should" indicates recommended procedures or practices that are discretionary.

BY ORDER OF THE DIRECTOR

GARY C. TUCKER
Colonel, USA
Staff Director, Administration

2 Encl
1. Storage and Handling of Compressed Gases and Liquids in Cylinders, and of Cylinders
2. Medical Gases and Gas Cylinders under Management of DPSC

DISTRIBUTION
Defense Logistics Agency: 1200
Army: 10
Navy: (two copies unless otherwise specified) A3 (OP 04; 09;94); C58F - Supply Corps School Det. C31C; C34C; FA5; FA6; FA7; FA10; FA18; FA23; FA24; FA27; FA32; FA39; FB6; FB7; FB10; FB13; FB21; FB28; FB29; FB30; FB31; FB34; FB41; FB45; FB48; FC4; FC5; FC7; FC12; FC14; FF1; FF5 (5 copies); FF49; FH1 FH4; FH13 ;FH30; FKA1A (10 copies); FKA1C (10 copies); FKA1G (SEA 56Y1 25 copies) FKA1F FKN1; FKN3; FKN5; FKN10; FKR1; FKR3 (less FKR3A); FKR3A (5 copies); FKR4; FKR7; FT (less FT1, FTL (5 copies); FT55; FT85; 21A; 27G (COM-NAVSUPPFORANTARCTICA only)copy to: (One copy each unless otherwise specified) A1 (SO-3, SO-4 only); A2A (NAVSCOMPT only); B5 (Commandant only) (5 copies); E3; ED1 (2 copies); FE1; FGL (2 copies): FN1 (2 copies) 24; 28; 29; 30; 31; 32; 36A; 39; 41 (less 41J and 41L)
Marine Corp: MARCORPS: L22 plus 7000176(4)/2191003 (1) less 7352007, 037, 040, 049; Copy to: 7000144, 146, 154, 158 (2) 8145
Air Force: F

COORDINATION: DLA-K, DLA-Q, DLA-S,
DLA-W, DLA-LP, DLA-LR,
DLA-AT
ARMY (ASQZ-PGP)(310-1t)),
NAVY (081B2/AN),
AIR FORCE (SAF/AADP),
MARINE CORPS (HQSP-3)

www.ingramcontent.com/pod-product-compliance
Lightning Source LLC
Chambersburg PA
CBHW081101290526
45795CB00006B/1942
9781491262542